PRAISE FOR

Who Is My Neighbor?

This is a great book that we will encourage all Bakke Graduate University staff, faculty and regents to get and read. It fact, it will encourage anyone who wants to follow Jesus.

Raymond J. Bakke
Chancellor and Professor of Urban/Global Leadership,
Bakke Graduate University

In *Who Is My Neighbor?* Dr. Wayne Gordon has drawn from more than 30 years of experience as pastor and teacher. The opening chapter is a page-turner and a provocative lead to a series of practical responses to Jesus' probing and ever-relevant question to everyone, especially the Church. Without a doubt, this is a timely text that seeks to discern the authentic presence of the divine in human interaction and interpersonal relationships.

Dr. Luis A. Carlo
Dean and Professor of Urban Studies and Religious Education
Alliance Theological Seminary

This is a timely message for our culture, and I can't think of a better person to deliver it. Wayne's life has truly been a sermon; he has lived out being a neighbor for more than 30 years in the great Lawndale Community in Chicago and in his friendship with me. This book will challenge you to think outside your comfort zone and see who your neighbors really are, and then to reach out in love. You'll be doing yourself —and those around you— a great favor by reading it.

Carey Casey
CEO of the National Center for Fathering, and Author of *Championship Fathering*

Who knew the story of the man beaten up by the side of the road in Jesus' teaching more than 2,000 years ago could be so relevant for us today? Wayne Gordon's insights in *Who Is My Neighbor?* is a must-read for those of us who love God and are committed to loving the poor as an expression of our Christian faith.

Noel Castellanos
CEO of Christian Community Development Association (CCDA)

Wayne Gordon writes as a father, as a football coach, as a pastor, as a neighbor, as an activist, as an economic developer . . . and as one who really believes Jesus meant the stuff He said. I have been sitting at the feet of Coach for nearly 20 years, gleaning his wisdom. This book is a gift to all of us.

Shane Claiborne
Author, Activist and Recovering Sinner (www.thesimpleway.org)

A generation ago, Howard Snyder wrote his classic book *Liberating the Church: The Ecology of Church and Kingdom*, a book which Donald G. Bloesch proclaimed was a "bold challenge to the church to abandon its preoccupation with its own preservation and to place itself in jeopardy for the sake of the lost and poor of the world." Wayne Gordon's *Who Is My Neighbor?* liberates *believers* for Kingdom purposes in this generation. We cannot love our neighbors until we recognize our neighbor. Gordon gently teaches us, through stories of redemption, how to *be* Christian and truly *live* again in a world that has pressed us to forget others in favor of preserving our own safety. May God give us courage to become the kind of people who see, stop, love, care for and redeem our neighbor.

Dr. Karen Walker Freeburg
Dean of Academic Programs, Northern Seminary

There is no one whose life qualifies him more to speak on principles of biblical neighborliness than Wayne "Coach" Gordon. He has been a godly neighbor to so many for so long that the revelatory lessons from his experience shine forth through *Who Is My Neighbor?*

Joseph Holland
Attorney, Entrepreneur and Founder of Holistic Hardware: Tools that Build Lives

Those who know Wayne Gordon know that his life can be summed up by saying, "He is a good neighbor." This jewel of a book is a guide to the Christian life forged in the crucible of real life on the real streets of the west side of Chicago. Gordie is "Coach," and everyone should read his playbook.

Glen Kehrein
Executive Director of Circle Urban Ministries

Who Is My Neighbor? challenges all serious followers of Christ to truly examine their hearts and hands as it pertains to their faith. Coach has put a challenging theological story into layman's terms, so there is no excuse for us not to know who our neighbor is. This is a roadmap for all of us who call ourselves followers of Christ!

Phil Jackson
Author, Senior Pastor of The House Hip Hop Church, and Associate Pastor of Lawndale Community Church

I've been waiting for the much needed, reality-grounded text on "neighboring 101." It's finally here. Thirty-plus years of front-line urban living have provided Dr. Gordon with practical, insightful, contemporary applications for the greatest command—to love God and love your neighbor.

Dr. Robert Lupton
Author, Founder and President of FCS Urban Ministries

Wayne Gordon has taken the Parable of the Good Samaritan and written a remarkable and wonderful book. Thanks to Gordie, I now know who my neighbor is. My neighbor is everyone, even those who are not yet Bears fans.

Pat McCaskey
Chicago Bears

I have long admired Wayne Gordon's commitment to "the least of these." His years with the mission and ministry of Lawndale Community Church are a living testimony of the Body of Christ at its best. They call him "Coach," and this book coaches people who really want to do the things that Jesus said. *Who Is My Neighbor?* tells powerful stories and reflections on Jesus' very challenging question. This is a very thoughtful and prayerful read that will help each one of us more fully live out Jesus' commandment to love our neighbors.

Jim Wallis
President of Sojourners, and Author of *God's Politics* and *Rediscovering Values*

DEDICATION

I dedicate this book to my wonderful wife, Anne.
We have partnered together for over 33 years. Anne and I share
life together; we do ministry, friends and family as one.
She is exceedingly and abundantly beyond what I ever hoped or
dreamed of in a wife. I shudder to think where I would be
without her. Anne is the love of my life, my best friend and
the collaborator of my soul.

LESSONS LEARNED
FROM A MAN
LEFT FOR DEAD

who is my neighbor?

WAYNE GORDON

Gospel Light

From Gospel Light
Ventura, California, U.S.A.

Published by Regal
From Gospel Light
Ventura, California, U.S.A.
www.regalbooks.com
Printed in the U.S.A.

Library of Congress Cataloging-in-Publication Data
Gordon, Wayne.
Who is my neighbor? : lessons learned from a man left for dead / Wayne Gordon.
p. cm.
ISBN 978-0-8307-5765-7 (trade paper)
1. Good Samaritan (Parable) 2. Church work. I. Title.
BT378.G6G67 2011
253—dc22
2010034854

2 3 4 5 6 7 8 9 10 11 12 13 14 15 / 20 19 18 17 16 15 14 13 12 11 10

Rights for publishing this book outside the U.S.A. or in non-English languages are
administered by Gospel Light Worldwide, an international not-for-profit ministry.
For additional information, please visit www.glww.org, email info@glww.org, or write
to Gospel Light Worldwide, 1957 Eastman Avenue, Ventura, CA 93003, U.S.A.

To order copies of this book and other Regal products in bulk quantities,
please contact us at 1-800-446-7735.

CONTENTS

FOREWORD

One of the things that I am most thankful for in life is that, during 50 years of ministry, I have lived at the mercy and goodness of my friends. I am filled with gratitude for the quality and depth of the friendships that God has given me.

Sometimes I get in trouble, though, when I start talking about my "best friend."

I've heard that Susanna Wesley—mother of John, Charles and several other children—was sometimes asked which one she loved the best. Her reply was something along the lines of, "It's the one who is away, until he comes back, and the one who is sick, until he is well." When people ask me who my best friend is, I have a similar answer: My best friend is the one I'm with right then. That person is the one with whom I'm enjoying fellowship, the one on which my attention is focused, and the one whom I'm especially grateful that God has brought into my life. As you can imagine, the trouble starts when I'm in a room with more than one friend at a time!

But there are a few special people who will always be at the top of my list of great friends. Wayne Gordon is one of those people. Gordy and I first met 28 years ago, and since then we have developed a deep, intimate friendship (his kids count me as one of their grandfathers) that has helped to sustain me as a person and has also undergirded the development of the Christian Community Development Association (CCDA)—an international ministry that equips thousands of Christians to incarnate the gospel in communities where hope is desperately needed.

One of CCDA's core principles is reconciliation. We believe that God is intent on reconciling all people to Himself—and to one another. I see my friendship with Gordy as fulfilling Paul's statement that "there is neither Jew nor Greek . . . for you are all one in Christ Jesus" (Galatians 3:28). I also see our friendship as a sign of God's blessing on the ministry He has graciously allowed us to undertake together.

I want to talk for a moment about Gordy as an ambassador of reconciliation. Here's this little white guy who moved into the inner city and became the best developer of indigenous leaders that I've ever known. Gordy's story proves that God can use anyone to break through barriers and do great things! The devil will try to tell you that God can't use you because of this or that—your skin color, your age and all sorts of other things—but that's a lie. Gordy certainly never believed it.

Gordy is a leader after God' own heart. Following Christ's example, he has chosen to make his home among people who are trapped and hurting, and he has committed himself to helping those people develop into whom God created them to be. If you ask Gordy whom he loves best, his neighbors in Lawndale will be right up at the top of his list. Oh, he loves people outside of Lawndale, too, but he loves the people in the community to which God has called him in a special way.

Jesus used the story of the Good Samaritan to teach us about who our neighbors are. Gordy has spent many years thinking about this story and applying it to his life and ministry. Now, as he shares his reflections and experiences, I believe God is going to use him to help the rest of us think more deeply about these very important questions: *Who is my neighbor?* and *How do I love my neighbor as I love myself?*

I recommend this book to anyone who is interested in understanding the transformative power of the gospel. I believe the main direction of the gospel is to develop people within communities, and this is Wayne Gordon's legacy. He has been a faithful ambassador of reconciliation, he has tirelessly discipled young leaders, and he has loved his neighbors completely. I am honored to call Gordy my friend, and I know we can all learn a lot from both his example and his words.

John M. Perkins
Co-founder and Chairman Emeritus of CCDA

NOTE TO THE READER

Understanding what God is trying to tell us constitutes one of the most challenging tasks facing the Church and individual believers. "Just follow the Bible" is easily said. It is far harder to accomplish. Sometimes we forget that the Bible was written in a different time and in a culture very different from ours. If we bring only our own Western cultural presuppositions or American values to our understanding of the Bible, we are almost sure to get it wrong more often than not.

This book focuses on a passage of Scripture found in Luke 10 that I believe the Church has by and large misunderstood, or at least failed to understand completely. More specifically, my focus is on the question, "Who is my neighbor?" It's an important question, one that has weighed heavily on my mind for many years. I'm convinced that if we attempt to answer this question only from the vantage point of our own predominant cultural experience, we will miss its many implications for how we should live our lives as Christians.

Let's take a closer look at this passage. Luke 10 features a person who is identified as "an expert in the law." The law in which he is an expert is not Roman law, but Old Testament law, which consists essentially of a very long list of rules—both "dos" and "don'ts." This list serves to remind us how much we need Christ, for it would be impossible to abide by all the commands cited in Old Testament law. In fact, there are 365 rules in the Old Testament that say, "Do not do something," and an additional 248 that say, "Do something." That adds up to 613 dos and don'ts.

I would venture to say that most Christians can't even name the Ten Commandments, let alone all those 613 rules. But the "expert" who is mentioned in Luke's Gospel very likely could recite all 613 backwards and forwards. Though he is not identified as such, the man was probably a Pharisee, since Pharisees made it their mission in life to become experts in the law. In fact, they memorized—word for word—the first five books of the Old Testament: Genesis,

Exodus, Leviticus, Numbers and Deuteronomy. So when Luke used the term "expert," he was not exaggerating in the least.

This expert, in Luke's account, sets out to test or trick Jesus. He begins by asking the question: "What must I do to inherit eternal life?" Jesus, apparently very aware of whom He is dealing with, responds in essence, "Why are you asking me? You're a teacher. You're an expert in the law. You've memorized the first five books of the Old Testament. You ought to know."

Here Jesus demonstrates a very useful teaching technique. Instead of just answering the question, He responds in a way that engages the inquisitor and gets him to think it through himself. Jesus asks, "What do you think?" to get the person talking a little bit. (Those of us who are teachers would do well to model this teaching method. Instead of just spoon-feeding people, we should attempt to get a conversation going.)

Responding to Jesus' question, the expert says, " 'Love the Lord your God with all your heart and with all your soul and with all your strength and with all your mind'; and, 'Love your neighbor as yourself.' "

Jesus acknowledges that the expert has answered correctly. Then He adds, "Do this and you will live."

The concept that the soul lives on after physical death was central to Old Testament Judaism (see Psalm 16:10; 1 Samuel 15:28; Isaiah 14:9-10). And the law was clear about what a person needed to do to gain eternal life. Of course, knowing what to do and actually doing it are two different things. In short, doing it perfectly is not possible.

I trust that most, if not all, who read these words understand that we inherit eternal life because we believe that Jesus Christ died for our sins. Thus, our inability to follow all those 613 Old Testament rules becomes irrelevant; our salvation is based not on our own righteousness, but on Jesus' righteousness.

The fact that we are saved through Christ, however, does not mean we shouldn't care about how we live as Christians. In fact, I think we should care even more. That is, in response to Jesus' sacrificial love, we ought to be highly motivated to live as Jesus would have us live. My point here is that there is a difference between being a Christian (and thus an inheritor of eternal life) and being a follower of Christ. Even though we are not able to do it perfectly, if we love God, we will strive to follow Him.

What stands out to me in the Pharisee's response (and in Jesus' affirmation of that response) is the connection between loving God and loving our neighbors. Central to genuinely obeying and following God is loving our neighbors as we love ourselves.

I'm convinced that truly loving our neighbors is the best way to respond to the biggest criticism non-believers have of the Church—one I'm sure you have heard—namely that Christians are a bunch of hypocrites. It's a criticism that we should take to heart, because sometimes it is accurate. Sometimes we believers live one way when we are in church or with fellow believers and another way when we think none of our brothers and sisters from church are watching.

According to Jesus, the real deal is the way we love on a daily basis. "Love the Lord your God with all your heart and with all your soul and with all your mind," He instructs, "[and] love your neighbor as yourself" (Matthew 22:37,39).

Scholars don't know if Jesus' words in Matthew 22 are based on the same incident that Luke writes about or if there were two separate incidents. There are a few small differences. In Matthew, Jesus answers the expert's question as opposed to responding with a question of His own. Also, in Luke, the word "strength" is included among the ways we should love the Lord; it does not appear in Matthew.

The main point, however, is totally clear: The most important commandments—the commandments that in some way encompass all the 613 Old Testament dos and don'ts—are to love God and to love our neighbors. In summarizing the law, Jesus took two Old Testament commands and put them together. The first is found in Deuteronomy 6:5: "Love the Lord your God with all your heart and with all your soul and with all your strength." The second is found in Leviticus 19:18: "Do not seek revenge or bear a grudge against one of your people, but love your neighbor as yourself. I am the Lord."

Jesus makes it clear in Matthew's Gospel that the second command is in no way subservient to the first. "The greatest command is to love God," He says, then adds in essence, "There's a second command that is equal in importance to the first, and that is to love your neighbor as you love yourself." He puts these two commands on the same plane.

At the church I have served for more than 30 years, we have strived to do ministry based on the strong conviction that those who would follow Christ are those who do their best to love their neighbors as themselves. The small group of high school kids who had the idea of starting this church was motivated by the goal of loving their neighborhood. All the ministries that over the years have emerged from Lawndale Community Church—including the health center, the development corporation, and all of the various programs for youth, those struggling with addiction, and others—are rooted in the goal of loving our neighbors.

But if we go further in Luke, we discover a passage that continues to challenge the people of Lawndale. It's a passage that I believe ought to challenge and motivate all who aspire to be Christ followers. We read in verse 29 that this expert in the law "wanted to justify himself, so he asked Jesus, 'And who is my neighbor?'"

The Pharisee, like virtually all human beings then and now, wanted to be justified, or validated. He figured he was doing all the things he was supposed to be doing, and he wanted to be acknowledged for his accomplishments. It's human nature to want to get credit for the good things we do, as opposed to doing them anonymously.

Specifically, the Pharisee wanted to be justified with respect to loving his neighbor. Again, he wanted to hear from Jesus that he was doing the right things. And then comes the crucial question. He asks Jesus, "Who is my neighbor?"

Now keep in mind that from the point of view of this expert in the law, this was at first merely a rhetorical question. That is, he already knew the answer (or thought he did). He just wanted to hear it from Jesus. Being Jewish, this Pharisee "knew" that his neighbors were fellow Jews—people who looked like him, thought like him, and worshipped the way he did.

Gentiles, on the other hand, were not to be considered neighbors. A Gentile is defined in the Bible as anyone who is not a Jew. Thus Europeans were Gentiles, as was anyone from Africa or Asia. Only those who came from one of the twelve tribes of Israel could be considered neighbors to this expert in the law. Little did the expert know that he was about to encounter a radically different understanding of "neighbor."

Instead of responding directly to the expert's question, Jesus tells a story. It's the parable of the Good Samaritan, a story that serves as the launching point for everything in this book because it is Jesus' response to the question, "Who is my neighbor?"

It goes like this:

A man was going down from Jerusalem to Jericho, when he fell into the hands of robbers. They stripped him of his clothes, beat him and went away, leaving him half dead. A priest happened to be going down the same road, and when he saw the man, he passed by on the other side. So too, a Levite, when he came to the place and saw him, passed by on the other side. But a Samaritan, as he traveled, came where the man was; and when he saw him, he took pity on him. He went to him and bandaged his wounds, pouring on oil and wine. Then he put the man on his own donkey, took him to an inn and took care of him. The next day he took out two silver coins and gave them to the innkeeper. "Look after him," he said, "and when I return, I will reimburse you for any extra expense you may have."

"Which of these three do you think was a neighbor to the man who fell into the hands of robbers?"

The expert in the law replied, "The one who had mercy on him."

Jesus told him, "Go and do likewise" (Luke 10:30-37).

From what we can tell, the expert in the law learned something that day. In his response to Jesus' final question, he conveyed a different understanding of "neighbor." No longer were his neighbors simply fellow Jews.

As Christians today, we need to consider how much we resemble the expert in the law who encountered Jesus more than 2,000 years ago. What is there for *us* to learn? To what extent do we define "neighbor" merely as those who live next door or on our block? To what extent have we been hypocritical as a result of not truly understanding that our neighbors are not only those who look like us, think like us, talk like us, act like us, and go to church with us?

We are *commanded* to love our neighbors as ourselves. How can we follow that command if we don't even know who our neighbors are?

This book represents more than 20 years of reflection, based on the parable of the Good Samaritan, which is Jesus' response to the question, "Who is my neighbor?" Each chapter focuses on some trait or characteristic that I hope will bring us to a truer understanding of who our neighbors are.

One suggestion I have is that you read this book slowly, perhaps even as slowly as a chapter a day during your devotions. It is also my hope that you will read this book with others and discuss these characteristics of our neighbors together. However you choose to read it, my prayer (and anticipation) is that this book will aid you as it has me in living out this part of the great commandment: to love our neighbors as we love ourselves.

Now, let's journey together as we seek to learn more about who, in our time, is most like that person who was beaten and left to die on the side of the road. Let's strive to be followers of Christ by learning more about whom and how we are to love as we consider the question, "Who is my neighbor?"

My Neighbor Is Hurting

One obvious characteristic of "my neighbor" is someone who is hurting. Clearly, in the account of the Good Samaritan, the man who was beaten up and left on the side of the road to die was hurting, both physically and emotionally.

Perhaps you or someone you know has experience with being mugged. But even if you don't, it's something we can all imagine. You're in the wrong place at the wrong time. You have something that somebody else wants. And the somebody who wants what you have is bigger and stronger than you are, or perhaps this person has some kind of weapon.

Maybe there is more than one person. They hit you until you can't defend yourself. They take your money, your cell phone, your credit cards, your shoes, and any clothes they think might fit them. They take your jewelry—your necklace and wedding ring. As a result, you are hurting, both physically from the beating and emotionally, because things that were dear to you have been lost forever.

In referring to the man who was hurting, Jesus is saying, "This is our neighbor; this is who I'm called to love." So it is for us. Our neighbors are people who are hurting. Perhaps they are hurting physically because of some accident. Perhaps they are hurting spiritually as they wrestle with some issue related to faith. Perhaps they are hurting emotionally—struggling to recover from some loss in their life.

Among children, the most typical kind of pain is physical. We can all remember the pain of a skinned knee or a bump on the noggin. Of course, children can also be exposed to emotional pain from a variety of sources, such as being teased or experiencing some kind of loss, perhaps the death of a pet or grandparent.

We try to shield our children from the pain they experience when they are ignored or belittled by their peers. "Sticks and stones can break my bones," we tell them, "but words will never hurt me." As we grow older, however, we know that this little ditty is simply not true. I've had my feelings hurt by other people's words; I suspect you have, too. Many of us, I'm sure, would gladly choose the pain of a broken leg over the pain from a broken relationship, from feelings of failure and low self-esteem, or from other people's words. Not to diminish the physical misery that many endure daily, but the emotional hurt that lies deep inside of us—the hurt that can't be healed by a cast or splint or more Ibuprofen—can for some be the worst kind of hurt.

Those among us who have experienced a particular kind of physical or emotional pain are more readily able to identify with others who are going through something similar. But even if we cannot understand fully what others are going through, we can understand what Jesus is saying to us, namely, "Those persons who are hurting are your neighbors. I want you to walk alongside them, to be there with them, to help them through their hurt in whatever way you can, to make a difference in their lives."

The young man who is struggling with depression is our neighbor. The single mom who just lost her job and doesn't know what to do next is our neighbor. The baby whose dad is in prison is our neighbor. The grandfather who is feeling lonely and isolated is our neighbor. So is the person who is going through a divorce and being attacked in court by someone he or she once loved as deeply as anyone.

We may not always know how to help. Sometimes we don't know what to say. But just to be there for a hurting person and to say we care can make a big difference.

Many churches have a time each week during worship for people to bring to God prayer concerns about those in the church or in their neighborhoods or places of work. This can be an opportunity to acknowledge and affirm that each person who is named—each man or woman or child who is hurting in some way—is our neighbor. In addition to praying for them, we have an opportunity—indeed a responsibility, if God is tweaking our hearts—to come to their aid in whatever ways we can.

We can't love our neighbors until we recognize them. So look around you. Be sensitive to those who are suffering—who are hurting—sometimes in silence. They will not be hard to find. And remember, that hurting person is your neighbor. Like the Good Samaritan, we have both the option to walk away and the opportunity to love.

My Neighbor Needs Help

A second obvious characteristic of a neighbor is somebody who needs help. This is a logical follow-up to the first characteristic, for, clearly, a person who is hurting is a person who needs help.

The parable of the Good Samaritan revolves around a person who needs help—who has been left naked and half dead and is unable to help himself. Each of those who traveled on that road had a choice as to whether or not to provide the help that was needed. In telling the story of the Good Samaritan, Jesus is saying to us that your neighbor and my neighbor are those people who need our help. And we have the opportunity, virtually every day of our lives, to witness for Christ by helping others.

On the surface, helping others seems like a very simple concept. It's not. Of course, if all we mean by helping others is opening the door for someone whose hands are full, that's one thing. But it's another thing if helping means that we have to get involved in another person's life, as the Good Samaritan did.

These days, people don't want to get involved. Perhaps they are afraid to get involved. After all, helping others can be a risky proposition. Besides, we have our own issues and problems, so we are hesitant to take on the problems of others.

Some people approach the question of helping others as if "help" were a limited commodity that has to be preserved. They are hesitant to help in some instances because they want to save their time and energy for bigger, more important problems. In contrast, I view "help" as a quality. It's an attitude that can be nurtured. The more we exercise our "help muscles," the more they will grow. With this view in mind, the goal is not to conserve our "help resources," but rather to grow them by cultivating an attitude of helpfulness.

If you have been hesitant or afraid to help others, perhaps you should start small. From time to time in my sermons, I challenge the young people in our congregation to look for ways, however small, to help others: "If you are walking home from school and you see an elderly woman trying to carry a couple of big bags of groceries, barely getting down the street, and she's got another two blocks to walk, young man—17 years old with muscles busting through your shirt—you go up to that woman and say, 'Excuse me, ma'am, may I carry these bags for you?'"

Sad to say, these days a woman in this situation might think she's about to have her groceries stolen. So I advise these young guys to offer to help as politely as possible: "Ma'am, I'm a Christ follower. I go to Lawndale Community Church, and I'd really love to help you by carrying those bags for you."

We need to remain aware of and open to the opportunities we have to help those who cross our paths unexpectedly. The Good Samaritan probably did not wake up in the morning expecting to come across someone who needed his help. But when the opportunity presented itself, he embraced it.

Helping others can also be premeditated. It certainly has been at Lawndale. The priority of helping others was established early in the life of our church. In fact, just a few weeks after we started the church, some high school kids approached me and said, "Coach, you know what? We said we're going to love God and love people, but we aren't doing anything for anybody in our neighborhood. Don't you think, as a church, we ought to love our neighborhood?"

It took me only a fraction of a second to realize that yes, of course, God calls churches to love their neighborhoods. We recognized that God was calling us, a little church of fifteen people, to start loving our neighborhood, even though we didn't know for sure where that commitment would lead.

Six years later, the health center came into existence. After that, we started a housing ministry to help people own their own homes or at least live affordably in better-quality rental units. We opened our Samaritan House to people who were homeless or on the verge of homelessness. We put them into apartments. They pay to live there, but they get the first three months' rent back so they can get started on a different path.

Many of our neighbors who need help are children. There's not a single public grammar school in North Lawndale where the majority of kids—that's 51 percent or more—read at grade-level. And we know if they can't read, they'll struggle to make it in our society. So every summer, we bring 125 grammar school kids to the church and help them learn to read.

We also have an after-school program with spots for about sixty kids. One of the little girls who came to the program many years ago grew up, got a college degree, and now serves as the program's director. We call this program Elevate, based on the goals of elevating the children's reading scores, math scores, language skills, interest in discovery, and artistic creativity, all as part of their striving for excellence.

Our neighbors are those persons—young, old and in between—who need help. They are people we see every day. As you seek to obey the great command to love your neighbor as you love yourself, put up your spiritual antennae and begin asking, "Who around me needs help?" Whoever it is, that person is your neighbor.

My Neighbors Are Those Who Cannot Help Themselves

You have probably heard of the ancient Italian city of Pompeii, best known for the huge volcano—Mount Vesuvius—that erupted there several centuries ago. No one was prepared, so as the layers of ash fell on it, the whole city was, in a sense, frozen in time, giving archaeologists a rare glimpse into what this city was like.

Not long ago, I got a report from a friend who'd taken a tour of Pompeii. On the tour, the group came across a wire fence, behind which were plaster casts of bodies that, according to the tour guide, were there when the ash covered them. The tour guide asked, "Do you know who these people were who didn't escape and were killed when the hot ash covered them?" Then the guide answered his own question: "They were slaves, trapped inside the fence so they couldn't get out."

Later they came across a wheat grinder and observed that a body had been chained to it. Again, the tour guide explained that slave masters typically chained their slave workers to their tools so they couldn't escape.

Suffice it to say that when Vesuvius erupted, many died because they were unable to help themselves. Some were fenced in or chained to something. Others got left behind because they didn't have horses or carriages or any other means of escape. In short, just like the man in Jesus' parable who was beaten up and left on the side of the road, they were unable to help themselves.

In 2005, we had our own version of Pompeii in America when Hurricane Katrina came ashore. Many people in New Orleans and in other places along the Gulf Coast lost their lives because they could not escape. Eighty percent of the people who lived in New Orleans had the means to evacuate. But 20 percent were at the mercy of others to help them. Upon a little bit of study, I discovered that 25 percent of households in New Orleans had neither a car nor access to one. Thus, they were unable to heed the warnings and help themselves.

Many people in our society today are unable to help themselves, not just when it comes to escaping a storm, but when it comes to succeeding—or in some cases just surviving—in our society. Of course, there are those who say that anyone can make it if he or she tries hard enough. "People are just lazy," the argument goes. "Why should anyone help them if they aren't willing to help themselves? They've just got to pull themselves up by their bootstraps."

There is some merit to this argument. In fact, when I speak to residents at our Hope House, a ministry for men who are trying to get their lives back together, I say to them point blank, "Some of you aren't going to make it because you're lazy. Some of you aren't going to make it because you're not going to do the things you need to do. You're just here for a free ride—for three squares a day and a bed."

I tell them this because I believe it's true. But it's not the total truth. Part of the truth, despite our country's cultural fascination with rugged individualism and pulling ourselves up by the bootstraps, is that some people are unable to do it on their own, no matter how hard they try. Too many people in both the political and Christian worlds ignore or play down this part of the truth.

I recall hearing the late evangelist Tom Skinner speaking one day about this whole bootstrap theory. "It's true," he said, "that people can pull themselves up by their bootstraps." Then he went on to say, "But for many people in our country who are trying to pull themselves up, somebody keeps cutting the bootstraps, and the people who are trying so hard fall back down."

To make a "thumbs up" or "thumbs down" judgment as to whether someone deserves help or is simply lazy is to grossly oversimplify the issue. The truth almost always lies somewhere between these two extremes. Certainly people can do more to help themselves. But that doesn't mean we can ignore the circumstances of their lives that have injured their spirits and sapped them of the strength they need to carry on as strongly as some think they should.

There are people in our society who have potential and drive but cannot make it because the public school education they received was inferior. They are unable to get into college or get a decent job because they never learned to read beyond a third- or fourth-grade level. There are people who grew up in broken homes and never learned essential life skills that many of us take for granted. Others suffer from depression or some form of mental illness. Still others have had their bootstraps cut so many times that they have very little energy left to press on.

As a society, we have allowed our hearts to become hardened to these people who need our help. To simply write all of them off as being lazy is to ignore the call of the gospel to love our neighbors. It's to abandon the responsibility that those of us who have been given much have to give to those who have been given little. I am reminded again of the common attitude of many toward those who were stuck on rooftops in the aftermath of Katrina: "It's not *my* responsibility to help them. It's the government's job."

In Ezekiel 16:49, the prophet elaborates on the sin of the city of Sodom, writing, "[They] were arrogant, overfed and unconcerned; they did not help the poor and needy." This sounds like those slave masters in Pompeii, and it sounds too much like contemporary America. The sin of Sodom and Gomorrah is the sin of many of us, and that is the sin of unconcern for other people.

We should be very careful about rushing to the judgment that those who live on the fringes of our society are simply lazy, so it's up to them to help themselves. Some of them are paralyzed because of the traumas they've had to endure in life. They need our help. Some have turned to drugs as an escape and are fighting this addiction. Yes, they have made mistakes. Who hasn't? Now, they want to help themselves, but to do that they need our help as well.

I have a friend who lives in New Orleans, Pastor John Gerhardt. When he heard about the coming storm, Pastor John didn't just get in his car and take off. Instead, he sent out the call to everybody in his church of 75 people and all of their friends. He told them to spread the word to come to the church, because they were going to evacuate as many people as they could. The lives of more than 100 people were saved because Pastor John and his family and others from the church thought not just about themselves, but also about helping those who were unable to help themselves.

Who do you know right now struggling with something in life and unable to help himself or herself completely or even in part? That person, Jesus said, is your neighbor. Go to that person. Yes, she needs to help herself. But she may need your understanding and your help to do just that.

4

My Neighbor Is Someone Who Appears on My Path

Christians are (or at least ought to be) by nature people who care deeply about the problems of our world. When we hear about human suffering—whether famine somewhere in Africa, typhoons in Southeast Asia, young men and women being killed or disfigured in Iraq, or miners trapped under the ground somewhere in the U.S.—we are affected and saddened by these human tragedies. We feel moved to pray for the victims, but we can also feel frustrated that there is little, if anything, more that we can do.

Especially for those who are particularly sensitive to human suffering, the problems of the world can at times seem overwhelming. Some people suffer from a mild but almost constant form of depression that is not rooted in anything that is happening in their own lives, but rather is a result of the general malaise of the world in which we live.

Thinking theologically for a moment, we must remember that this is a fallen world. We see daily reminders of this reality in our newspapers and on the TV news that we are not in heaven, but on earth. Our world is a place where evil and tragedy are present, often nearer to us than we would like. There is plenty of bad to go with the good—lots of suffering amid the joy.

We can at times be so burdened by the problems of the world that we feel paralyzed—unable to help, unable to act. Because we can't do everything, we end up not doing anything, despite the fact that we truly care and genuinely desire to help in some way.

With this in mind, the story of the Good Samaritan can function as a source of comfort. It can help us realize that we are not responsible for solving all the world's problems, thus freeing us to act when we have the opportunity. "Opportunity" is the operative word. Who are our neighbors? Our neighbors are those who appear on our paths, thus giving us an *opportunity* to help them.

In the parable of the Good Samaritan, we can reasonably assume that none of the three people who found a man beaten by the side of the road had awakened that morning intent on going out and solving one or more of the world's big problems. They were each merely going about their business for that day when an opportunity they had not anticipated landed on their path, literally. Two of them declined to act on this opportunity; the Good Samaritan chose to seize it.

One of the greatest challenges facing preachers and Christian teachers is to exhort followers of Christ to do what they can do without making them feel guilty for not doing what they can't do. Too many people feel guilty for, or at least troubled by, not doing anything about problems they cannot do anything about—for not helping people they are not in a position to help.

Imagine someone in the community has a child who was injured. Their insurance payments have run out. They need a million dollars. I know many Christians who are so caring that they would donate the million dollars in a second, no questions asked. The problem is they don't have it to give. The best they can do is donate 10 or 15 dollars and perhaps help organize a fundraiser.

Around the country and all over the world, every day—every second in fact—someone is facing a crisis. An elderly person falls and breaks a hip, a young mother is diagnosed with cancer, a family loses their home to a fire or to a mortgage payment they can't make. These stories grieve us, but the reality is that none of us is Superman. We have neither the opportunity nor the ability to solve all of these problems.

We need to simplify our Christian living. Instead of being overwhelmed by problems we cannot solve, we need to pay attention to those people and those opportunities God has placed on our paths. Who are the people whom God allows you the privilege of coming into contact with on a regular basis? Those persons are your neighbors. It's that simple.

These neighbors don't necessarily have to live next door or even on your street. They could be children or families in another part of the world who somehow landed on your path, and with whom you have built a long-distance relationship. The main point is that once we are freed of the burden of feeling that we have to solve *all* the world's problems, we are better able to notice the opportunities that surround us. We are free to experience the joy that comes from serving others—the same joy the Good Samaritan must have felt from giving help and comfort to someone in need.

I don't ever want anyone to feel guilty. But I do want to challenge followers of Christ to heed the example of the Good Samaritan. My church participates in the Angel Tree program, which provides Christmas gifts for children whose moms or dads are incarcerated. There are 1,500 children in our neighborhood who have a parent in prison, and we don't have anywhere near that number of people in our church. And many in our congregation don't have the spare income to purchase a gift on their own. Still, we challenge everyone not to walk by the sign-up table without stopping to think about what they might be able to do. If they can't buy a gift on their own, we suggest they go in with two or three other families.

I know of a pastor who, during the morning service, allows people to mention some of the needs of which he is aware. For example, an elderly woman needs a ride to a doctor's appointment later in the week. Or someone has just had a child, and the family could use a few home-cooked meals. During the service, the pastor asks for people to commit right then and there to meeting these needs. There are several hundred in attendance, and he refuses to believe that there aren't at least a few who are able to respond to each of the needs. If no one does, he'll say (somewhat jokingly but getting his point across), "This service is not going to end until I have my volunteers. I'll preach all afternoon if I have to!" Then the hands start going up.

Sometimes the simplest acts of kindness—a card for someone in the hospital or for the new family in town that is still trying to make friends and find their way—can be the most meaningful. Some time back, I had surgery and had to be in the hospital. Each of the children from our after-school program sent me a card. I read every one of those cards, and they made me feel great.

Each morning, I spend a little time reading the Bible and praying. Every day, I give my life back to Jesus. I say, "Lord, take me, use me. What is it You want me to do today?" And God brings onto my path—brings to my mind—somebody to call on the phone or reach out to in some other way.

God will do the same for you. Don't be burdened by problems that you can't do anything about. But look for someone on your path whom you have the opportunity to help. That person is your neighbor.

5

My Neighbor Is Someone Who Has Been Robbed

A few years ago, our church welcomed six young women who were part of the Mission Year program. These women had devoted a year of their lives to mission work in the city of Chicago. One Sunday afternoon, they were on their way to a train station to attend a Mission Year team meeting when a couple of young men approached them with a gun and demanded everything they had: their purses, their cell phones, their money, and all other valuables. Fortunately, the women were not physically harmed, though this was obviously a very traumatic experience.

Those who live in urban environments in our country are more familiar with assault than they would like to be. Most people who live in the city, if they have not been robbed themselves, know someone who has been. In fact, once there was a robbery at gunpoint at the barbershop where my son and I get our hair cut.

Whether or not a gun is involved, people who are robbed feel violated. Certainly that must have been how the man on the road from Jerusalem to Jericho felt. It's a very humbling and demeaning thing to be robbed. Something that is yours—something you've earned and have a right to possess—is taken away. People who have been robbed feel many different emotions, including anger and fear. Depending on the specifics, it can take them a very long time to deal with the psychological fallout from being assaulted.

Robbery is not just about material possessions. People get robbed in many different ways. People can feel robbed of their dignity based on the color of their skin or the work they do or the clothes they wear or the neighborhood in which they live. Many women feel robbed as a result of being treated like second-class citizens based on their gender. Those who have been robbed of their dignity sometimes have trouble acknowledging that, regardless of where they live or what they wear or how they look, they bear the image of their Creator.

People can get robbed in subtle ways. Consider, for example, the faithful employee who is promised a raise after three months of showing up at work on time and doing a good job. The raise never comes. Sometimes robbery is perfectly legal.

People are also robbed of the truth. I won't forget a day many years ago when I was driving in the city. While I was stopped at a traffic light, a man came up to my window holding a little container and asking for a donation to his church's ministry. My inclination was to help until he told me that he was part of the Unification Church (followers of Sun Myung Moon).

This brought to mind my college days, when I visited Korea with other students from Wheaton College. I was standing at the front of a public bus when I noticed a picture of Jesus by the driver. I got the driver's attention, then pointed to the picture of Jesus, and then to my heart. He broke into a big smile. Just a few minutes later, the bus driver became agitated and began repeating the same word very loudly. Finally I asked if anyone could tell me what he was talking about. As it turns out, he was pointing to a Unification Church, and the word he was repeating was "Satan."

Back to that street corner in Chicago: There was no way I was going to give that young guy any money. But I didn't hate him.

I remember thinking that this man had been deceived. He was probably sincere—and well-meaning—but he had in essence been robbed of the truth. So, drawing from the Sermon on the Mount, I said to him, "You know what? Jesus said that we are to seek the truth. If you seek, you shall find." I added, "Don't just believe everything you hear. Please seek the truth. I'm going to pray for you. God bless you."

When Jehovah's Witnesses or people from other misguided religious groups come knocking on our doors or meet us at the supermarket, we need to understand that they are like that beaten man on the side of the road. They have been robbed. They are our neighbors; we're called to love them and to help them find the truth.

It's not just cults that have robbed people of the truth. People are also robbed by our materialistic society into thinking that money and possessions are pretty much all that matters. People are robbed by advertisements that tell us our self-image is based on the cars we drive or the vacation spots we frequent. People are robbed by some of the messages put forth by the entertainment industry—that might makes right, and that external beauty counts for everything.

Some of these people are very wealthy and may seem content, even happy. But even though they don't fit the stereotype of an assault victim, they have been robbed. "The god of this world has blinded the unbelievers' minds that they should not discern the truth" (2 Corinthians 4:4, *AMP*). Do you know someone who has been blinded—robbed of the truth by the god of this world? It might be someone who lives next door, someone from work, a soccer mom, or the parents of one of your child's friends. That person is your neighbor.

I'm glad to say that the story of those Mission Year workers has a happy ending. In fact, it has become a sort of signature testimony for what Lawndale Community Church is all about. I was not in Lawndale at the time the assault took place. I was at least a couple of hours away when someone called to tell me what had happened. So I started calling people—everyone I could think of—to tell them to get over there and offer comfort and support to those young women who had been assaulted.

When I got back into the neighborhood, I called the women and told them I would be there in five minutes. Using the nickname I am known by, the woman who answered the phone responded, "Well, Coach, you don't really need to come now. We're fine."

Surprised, I asked, "What do you mean?"

She replied, "Well, the bottom line is that for the last two hours, our doorbell has not stopped ringing."

Because the word had gone out to all of our church family, dozens upon dozens of people came over to offer their support. The woman estimated the number to be well over 100. These women felt loved, and they found a certain sense of safety and security to counteract the effects of the assault. I was so proud of the people of the church for recognizing who their neighbors were and for responding so quickly.

When I got back in the neighborhood, I went over to see how the Mission Year team was doing, even though I wasn't really needed. And I'm glad I did, because I had the chance to talk with the next-door neighbor, who by then knew the story of what had happened to those young women. He said to me, "I've lived here all my life, and I have never seen anything like this. If I counted up all the people I know, it's not as many as those who came to visit today."

Who do you know who has been robbed? That person is your neighbor. Reach out and offer your love. And remember that your action may benefit more than just that person, because you never know who might be watching and might be drawn closer to Christ because of your example.

6

My Neighbor Is Someone Who Is Half Dead

The Bible tells us that the man who was on his way from Jerusalem to Jericho was beaten until he was "half dead." These were not mere surface injuries. He had more than just a few scrapes, bumps and bruises. He was halfway to death, and most likely *would* have died had not someone intervened on his behalf.

Our neighbors are those people around us who are, in some way, half dead. They need someone to intervene as the Good Samaritan did. They need someone to help them go from being half dead to being fully alive.

There are many ways in which a person can be half dead. Someone whose heart stops beating might be halfway to physical death, at least until another person intervenes by doing CPR and then getting the ailing person to a hospital so that life can make a comeback. Those who are on life support might be considered half dead because they need machines to keep them breathing and tubes to provide the nutrition required to sustain what life they have.

And then there are those who are spiritually or emotionally half dead, or in many cases more than half dead. These people are our neighbors. They need some kind of resuscitation—some kind of life support—that ambassadors for Christ can and ought to provide.

In his letter to the Ephesian church, Paul writes, "As for you, you were dead in your transgressions and sins" (Ephesians 2:1). Do you know people who are half dead because they are struggling with sin in their lives and have not yet experienced the freeing power of Jesus Christ? Those persons are your neighbors.

A man who lives in the Lawndale community provides a perfect example of someone reaching out to a neighbor who was half dead. This man, Mr. Harris, was once the topic of a wonderful feature in the *Chicago Tribune*. The article chronicled how Mr. Harris, back in the '70s, lost his job when the company he worked for was sold. Instead of giving up, he started his own business, Harris Ice Company, which went on to become an extremely successful business in Chicago. And Mr. Harris made it a point to hire people in his community who needed jobs.

Mr. Harris is a deacon in a church in another part of Chicago. Going in early on Sunday mornings to open the church, for several weeks in a row he noticed a young man standing on a corner nearby. Each week, when Mr. Harris tried to get his attention, the young man would run away, a tell-tale sign that he was doing what too many young men are doing on the street corners of our cities: selling drugs. For all intents and purposes, this young man was half dead.

I am reminded of an exchange that well-known African-American mentor and educator Juwanza Kunjufu had one day with a young drug dealer in Los Angeles. Kunjufu was trying to talk this young man out of selling drugs, not an easy task since sellers could make two or three thousand dollars a week. Kunjufu asked the young man to think about his future. He specifically asked him if he knew what anyone who had been selling drugs 10 years ago was doing today. The young drug dealer paused for a moment and then said, in essence, "I can't think of anybody that's doing anything. Everybody I can think of is either in prison, strung out on drugs themselves, or dead."

Kunjufu responded, "Well, then, there isn't much future in what you're doing if you're probably not going to be here 10 years from now. You're half dead already."

The saddest part of this exchange was the young man's response: "Yeah, but if I have to go back to life the way it was before I started selling drugs, I'd rather be dead."

But Mr. Harris did not give up. One day, when he went in to open up the church, instead of just hollering at the young man, he snuck up behind him and grabbed him so he couldn't run away. He started a conversation with this young drug dealer/gangbanger. And pretty soon he offered the young man a job. Mr. Harris said, "I can't pay you what you might be able to make doing what you're doing now, but I can offer you a future. I want you to come and work for me." The young man showed up for work the next day, and at last report is still doing well. He's on his way from being half dead to being fully alive.

There are people all around us who are half dead. Some may be half dead physically; they need people to visit them in the hospital or in their homes. But there are many more who are half dead in other ways. Some kind of addictive behavior or mental illness or emotional depression is keeping them from being as alive as they want to be and ought to be. Perhaps they are still stuck in their sins and need someone to introduce them to Jesus in a way that truly reveals His unending mercy and compassion.

Ephesians 2:5 tells us that God "made us alive with Christ even when we were dead in transgressions—it is by grace you have been saved." We need to resuscitate people in our communities who are half dead and who don't know Jesus Christ. For, truly, they are our neighbors.

7

My Neighbor Is Someone Who Is Naked

Among the things the robbers did to the man who was going down from Jerusalem to Jericho was to strip him of his clothes. Anyone who walked by after this man had been beaten and robbed could plainly see that he was naked.

Nakedness is arguably the ultimate metaphor for human vulnerability and humiliation. To be naked is to be totally exposed—defenseless, deprived of dignity, and totally at the mercy of others.

In the Bible, as early as the second chapter of Genesis, we get an idea of the significance of nakedness. God created Adam and Eve in their "birthday suits." And unless there is something very unusual about you, you entered this world in the same state of nakedness.

For the first human beings, nakedness was not initially a problem. It was not a source of embarrassment or shame. Then sin came into the world, and Adam and Eve were instantly exposed—deprived of the dignity they once enjoyed in the Garden. For the first time, they knew what it was like to feel humiliation and vulnerability. They were naked and ashamed.

I am well acquainted with the shame associated with physical nakedness. I've walked into hospital rooms where the person I am visiting is partly sedated or has limited ability to move. A part of his or her body that is normally not exposed is visible, and my instinct is to ask for a nurse to come in and cover it up, or I might do it myself as discreetly as I can.

Also, my mother suffered from Alzheimer's disease. Not long ago, I was visiting her, and I told her it was time for her to take a shower and get ready for bed. So she went into the bathroom and took off her clothes. Then I heard her say, "I can't turn on the shower." I wanted to help her, but I did not want her to feel the embarrassment of her son seeing her naked. Maybe with her Alzheimer's she wouldn't know it, but to me her dignity was at stake. I knew where the shower was, so I opened the door and backed in. I was able to turn the shower on and wait until the water was warm, then leave without seeing her.

What we must realize, however, is that nakedness is not confined to the physical—to being without clothes. As noted above, nakedness is a metaphor for being totally unprotected, destitute and defenseless. The things in our lives that get exposed, even though we don't want them to, go far beyond our physical bodies. When others find out about a family problem—an alcoholic father or a teenager with a drug problem—we feel exposed.

I know people who don't want any visitors to come to their house because of the way the house might look. Perhaps they have trouble keeping it clean. Maybe they can't afford to fix the broken toilet or replace the worn carpeting. If someone stops by unannounced, they feel exposed. Now, someone knows something about them that they didn't want the other person to know.

We all are prone to hide behind various masks or behind social and psychological "clothing" because we are afraid to be naked in the presence of others. We don't want them to see us as we really are; we don't want them to know about the spiritual or emotional struggles we face (even though chances are they face many of the same things).

Perhaps you have been in a position where you got caught up in the moment and became vulnerable by exposing some deep part of your life that, upon later consideration, you're not so sure you ought to have exposed. Once these things are opened up, they don't seem to ever close. When I've done this, I always feel a bit awkward the next time I see the person. I can't help but wonder if they're thinking about what I told them, and as a result I feel exposed—emotionally naked.

Who is my neighbor? It is that person who is naked—defenseless and vulnerable. It's the woman who is too embarrassed to tell anyone that her son is in prison. It's the family that can't afford to pay their electric bill. It's the young man who was sexually molested and doesn't know whom to go to for help. It's the seemingly well-adjusted dad who's afraid to admit that he struggles with depression. They are our brothers and sisters, our friends and co-workers. If we look more closely, we might be able to see their nakedness.

We have something to learn from how God responded to the nakedness of Adam and Eve. In His tender way, He provided a little garment for each of them and said, "Here. Put this on. I still love you, and I don't want you to be exposed."

There are a lot of naked people in our lives. They may not be without clothes, but they have in some way been stripped of their dignity, stripped of who they are as human beings, and limited in some way from being all they ought to be and can be. They need someone to come alongside who simply will not allow them to feel embarrassed, but who instead will affirm their dignity and provide the same kind of tender, loving care offered to the man who, many years ago, went down from Jerusalem to Jericho.

8

My Neighbor Is Someone Who Is Unable to Ask for Help

Some people have no trouble asking for help when they need it. Perhaps the most obvious example is the beggar. Anyone who's ever been to a city of pretty much any size has encountered people looking for a handout.

Many of those who have resorted to outright asking other people for some of their money have turned begging into something of an art form by adopting some very subtle strategies with proven records of success. A friend informed me of one such strategy where the person asks for a mere eight cents in order to buy a train ticket. (Of course, anyone would be willing to give someone eight cents, figuring if he's asking for less than a dime, he must be sincere.) But then, once the change is out of the pocket, the "solicitor" says, "No, I said *eighty* cents." The ploy works because once someone has made an initial commitment to help, it's hard to back out.

Another form of psychological manipulation is the "God Bless You" technique.

One person walks by and doesn't put anything into the cup. But the beggar says, "God bless you" anyway. His words don't change the first person's mind, but the next guy walking by hears how gracious the beggar was to a non-contributor and feels obligated to reach into his pocket for a little change.

The culture of begging here in the U.S. is nothing compared to what one encounters in Islamic countries. That's because one of the Five Tenets of Islam is giving alms to the poor. I recall the time I visited Egypt. Whenever I was near a mosque, I would see dozens upon dozens of beggars out there waiting so that, by being on the receiving end, they could help their Muslim brothers fulfill the command to give alms to the poor.

People resort to begging for a variety of reasons. Some no doubt are perfectly capable of finding a job and fending for themselves. Others have been so beaten down by life—have tried and failed so many times—that they don't know what else they can do.

Regardless of the reasons, at least those who beg on the streets have the ability to ask for help. But let's think about those in our world who do not have this ability. The man who was beaten while on his way from Jerusalem to Jericho ought to remind us of such persons. He was in pain, unable to stand on his own, perhaps unable to move or even to speak. He was totally dependent on someone else noticing that he needed help.

If only we look around, we will find people who, for a variety of reasons, are unable to ask for help. I recall on one occasion pulling into a gas station to fill up. I saw someone I recognized a couple of pumps over. It was a pastor from another church—an African-American gentleman who had befriended me in the early days of my ministry and had always been kind to me.

But now he was getting up in years and, though he could still function, was beginning to struggle with some form of dementia. We exchanged smiles, but I could tell he was having trouble figuring out how to get his credit card to work at the gas pump. Even after I was done filling up, he was still fumbling around, trying to get started. He needed help, but was unable to ask for it. I didn't want to go over to him and say, "Hello, pastor. Let me do that for you." That might make him feel bad. But neither could I just get back in my car and drive away, since I knew he needed assistance. I prayed silently, "God, how can I help this man without stripping him of his dignity?"

Finally I called his name, and as I walked toward him, he waved back at me and called my name. I was glad that he remembered me. We shook hands, and then it came to me that it might help if I blamed the gas pumps for his struggles. So I said, "Man, these pumps are really hard to figure out, aren't they? I can never remember which way my card is supposed to go in, you know? Today I must have gotten lucky."

This enabled him to say, "You know, I'm having that problem right now."

To which I responded, "Really? Hmm. Well, I just got mine going. Would you like me to try your card?"

He said, "Sure." So I took his card and put it in and pulled it out, and he was able to pump his gas.

God had given me the wisdom to do the right thing in that moment. This man was my friend and my neighbor. If I had just minded my own business and stayed on the sidelines, I never would have helped him, because he didn't ask for my help.

Our world is full of people who need help but are unable to ask for it. When I think about who these people are, the two groups that come first to my mind are the very old and the very young. As was the case with my friend at the gas station, many older persons who once were able to care for themselves (and perhaps for others) now find it difficult to accept that they need to depend on other people for many things—moving furniture, paying bills, getting to the doctor's office, shoveling snow, and more.

Then there are the young people—the children who have yet to develop the words or the understanding even to know they need help, let alone how to ask for it. I think especially of those who have never experienced what a healthy family is like—children who have been neglected, if not abused, and who have no way of knowing that children are supposed to receive help from the adults in their lives.

One of the ways that several families at Lawndale Community Church have reached out to the voiceless is by opening their homes to at-risk children through a program called Safe Families, coordinated by Lydia Children's Home in Chicago. The program helps children whose families are, for any number of reasons, unable to care for them, at least temporarily. The Miller family in our church once had five children come to their home—an infant boy (six months old) and four others ranging in age from two to five years old.

This kind of ministry can be challenging, because, coming from unstable homes, these children often bring their difficulties and struggles along with them. This can be a great source of stress for families. And yet people who feel called to this kind of ministry typically experience a deep-seated joy that comes from responding to the Lord's tug on their hearts to be a neighbor to someone in need—to someone who is vulnerable and who has no voice.

In Proverbs 31:8-9, we read: "Speak up for those who cannot speak for themselves, for the rights of all who are destitute. Speak up and judge fairly; defend the rights of the poor and needy."

By His telling of the parable of the Good Samaritan, Jesus is calling us to do the same. Voiceless people need us, for we live in a society where it's the "squeaky wheel" that gets the grease. Those who complain the most loudly are most likely to get what they want. People with power and money (usually the two go together) call the shots. Thus, to be a voice for the voiceless is inherently countercultural.

It's been said that the best measure of a society's morality is how it treats its weakest and most vulnerable people. So as we reach out to the voiceless among us, not only are we bringing comfort and hope to individuals, but we are also doing our part, however small it may seem, to build a better world.

Who are those around you who have lost their voices, or who perhaps never had voices to lose? The children, the elderly, the disabled, and those who struggle with emotional or mental illness are some that may fall into this category. Jesus has helped us to understand that our neighbors are those who need our help even when they are unable to ask for it.

9

My Neighbor Is of a Different Race

Virtually all Bible scholars agree that the man who was beaten up and left to die on the side of the road was Jewish. He was of a different race than was the man who stopped to help him. This fact is extremely important if we truly want to understand Jesus' parable of the Good Samaritan in a way that changes our lives.

I don't use the word "hate" lightly, but the fact is that, in Jesus' time, Jews hated Samaritans. A brief history lesson helps us understand why. During the exile, as God's chosen people were taken out of Israel, God commanded them not to intermarry among those who worshipped other gods. But some Jewish people paid no heed. They intermarried, and a new, mixed-race ethnic group was born.

Jews hated Samaritans, and in time Samaritans learned to hate back. We've seen it time and time again throughout history in all parts of the world: Cultural groups seem to reserve their greatest hatred for other groups that are closely related, but not exactly the same.

For people in Jesus' day to hear that it was a despised Samaritan and not a fellow Jew who stopped to help this Jewish man was astounding, inconceivable, unthinkable. It's no wonder Jesus was considered a radical.

More than 2,000 years after Jesus gave us this parable, racial conflict continues to plague our world. Most wars around the globe—in Bosnia, Northern Ireland, Myanmar, Sri Lanka and elsewhere—are rooted in conflict between ethnic groups. In recent years in Darfur, Rwanda and Nigeria, hundreds of thousands of black Africans have been murdered by fellow black Africans.

Our country, of course, has its own checkered history when it comes to race relations. There are those who yearn longingly for the religion of our "Founding Fathers."

But when my good friend and community development pioneer John Perkins hears this, he responds, "I'd have to be a fool to want to go back there. Because if we'd go back to the religion of our Founding Fathers, I'd be a slave."

Racism in the U.S. today is far more subtle than it is in some other places around the world. In their book *Divided by Faith*, authors Michael Emerson and Christian Smith provide insight into the U.S. racial divide that is nothing short of profound. In fact, Bill Hybels, founding pastor of Willow Creek Community Church, has said this book wreaked havoc on his life by bringing to light the racial divide, particularly between black people and white people, in America.

Because the word "racism" is such an explosive, divisive and broad term, Emerson and Smith in writing their book came up with a new phrase. They speak of America as a "racialized society."

In essence, in a racialized society, ethnic groups are not in open war against one another, but they remain separated in significant ways. Interethnic and interracial marriages are very rare in a racialized society. And the different groups live in their own, separate areas. You will find this in virtually all U.S. cities. Some areas are predominantly Puerto Rican or Mexican or African-American or European-American. We rarely interact in any significant ways with people of other groups. Even in the church, 90 percent of African-Americans worship in predominantly African-American churches, while 95 percent of white churchgoers attend predominantly white churches.

In the mid-'70s, long before the term "racialized society" was coined, I experienced first-hand its reality. After I took a job as a teacher and coach at a Chicago high school, I began looking for an apartment not far from the school. I wanted my new home to serve as a sort of base for ministry among the young men I was teaching and coaching. I found an apartment about a block away from the school, but did not rent it because the manager said black kids would not be allowed into the building.

When I looked into another apartment building in an area where lots of black people lived, the manager said to me, "We're all colored in this building, and we don't mix here." This time I didn't give up. I talked my way into a place in that building. The woman, Mrs. Washington, eventually became one of my best friends. She cooked dinner for me almost every night and invited me over to watch Monday Night Football since I didn't have a TV. Nevertheless, her initial response reflected a prevailing attitude.

Not much has changed in 30-plus years. We are still struggling as a society and as Christians with how to do better. I've observed that some of us white folks feel we have "arrived" when we say to other people, "I'm colorblind. I don't see you as a black person or a Latino person or a Middle Eastern person. You're just like I am."

However, I've come to understand that to be "colorblind" should not be the goal. For one thing, God made us multicultural and multiracial. We are enriched by diversity and ought to celebrate it. For another thing, if we are blind to racial and ethnic differences we will also likely be blind to the inequalities associated with these differences.

One recent study established that black people were getting paid two-thirds as much as white people for doing exactly the same job. And, while selling five grams of crack cocaine is enough to send a person to prison for five years, it takes 500 grams of powder cocaine to bring about the same sentence. Since crack cocaine users are predominantly black, and powder cocaine users are largely white and Hispanic, this disparity in the mandatory minimum sentences lands a disproportionate number of young black males in jail. A few years ago, in the dark of night, some athletic directors from Chicago-area high schools organized their athletic conferences in such a way as to leave out all the black schools. (As a result of a lawsuit, this did not go through, but the sentiment that lies behind such an attempt cannot be ignored.)

Attempting to be colorblind is likely to result in ignoring inequities in areas such as education and housing. We also run the risk of being blind to the race-based discrimination that continues to plague our country in the social arena.

Harvard and Princeton professor Cornel West, author of the book *Race Matters,* has told the story of how he waited in Manhattan while nine empty cabs passed him by, only to witness a tenth cab stopping shortly after passing him to pick up a woman who'd just walked out of her Park Avenue apartment. As she entered the cab, the woman looked back at Dr. West, realizing what had just happened. She called the situation "ridiculous," but that didn't stop her from getting in the cab.

In his letter to the Galatians, Paul addresses Christ followers who are struggling with issues of race. He tells them that in Christ Jesus "there is neither Jew nor Gentile" (Galatians 3:28, *TNIV*). Paul's message for us today would be that in Christ Jesus there is no black, white, Mexican, Puerto Rican, Cuban, Colombian, Middle Eastern, Argentine or Chinese. We are all one in Christ Jesus.

I believe that it's an abomination to God that we've got a black church, a white church, a Chinese church, a Mexican church, and many other ethnic-specific Christian assemblies. I believe further that for Christ followers, mending our racialized society ought to be a priority. We need to have the same sense of urgency that Martin Luther King Jr. demonstrated in "A Letter from a Birmingham Jail." This letter was addressed not to overt racists, but to eight white clergymen who were calling for racial harmony. Yet these eight pastors had chastised Dr. King for taking his message to the streets instead of allowing things to run their course in the court system. King's message, in essence, can be summarized by a short line from the letter: "To wait means never will it happen."

We need to begin doing what we can to rewrite stories such as the one shared by Cornel West. When we see that a cabbie has passed up someone from a minority group, we need to say, "No. That's not gonna happen on my watch." And then give that cab ride to the person who was there first.

This would be a good start. Of course, there is much, much more we need to do to rework the structures and attitudes of our racialized society. It all begins with recognizing that for the Good Samaritan, race didn't matter. The only thing that mattered was that the man who had been victimized and needed help was his neighbor.

My Neighbor Is a Stranger

We say to our children, as well we should, "Don't talk to strangers. Stay away from people you don't know." We do this to protect our children. Young people inherently trust other people; they assume the best in others instead of the worst. They have not yet become cynical, as many adults have. We need to learn from the children among us, but we also need to protect them from the evil in the world that they are too young and innocent to recognize. So we say to them, "Don't talk to strangers."

When we get older, however, we need to be careful about taking this advice too seriously, for our neighbors are strangers—people who are unfamiliar to us and who may also seem a little strange to us. The man who was beaten up and left to die on the side of the road was a stranger to those who walked by that day. They didn't know him. But in the case of the Good Samaritan, not knowing this man did not stop him from offering help.

Mature persons in Christ are no longer children. We have the ability to discern when a situation is safe enough to intervene and offer our help to a stranger in need.

Jesus makes it perfectly clear that serving "the least of these" is tantamount to serving Him:

> Then the King will say to those on his right, "Come, you who are blessed by my Father; take your inheritance, the kingdom prepared for you since the creation of the world. For I was hungry and you gave me something to eat, I was thirsty and you gave me something to drink, I was a stranger and you invited me in, I needed clothes and you clothed me, I was sick and you looked after me, I was in prison and you came to visit me."
>
> Then the righteous will answer him, "Lord, when did we see you hungry and feed you, or thirsty and give you something to drink? When did we see you a stranger and invite you in, or needing clothes and clothe you? When did we see you sick or in prison and go to visit you?"
>
> The King will reply, "I tell you the truth, whatever you did for one of the least of these brothers of mine, you did for me" (Matthew 25:34-40).

I've been a pastor for a long time, but I'm still learning to be a better neighbor to the strangers with whom I cross paths. Not long ago, I was preparing a sermon focusing on the above passage. On the Saturday before the sermon, my son, Andrew, and I made a trip to a Walgreen's drugstore. As we were going in, we noticed a man outside on crutches. He had only one leg. He was a stranger. He didn't say anything to us—he didn't ask for help. We walked by him without another thought.

But someone who was walking behind us talked to the man. He asked him, "Are you thirsty? What would you like to drink?" When I heard those words "thirsty" and "drink," the passage I'd been reflecting on all week came to mind. I was going to be preaching on it, but the guy who was literally a step behind me was a step ahead when it came to reaching out to a stranger.

Andrew and I got what we'd come to get. But as we were approaching the checkout line, we looked at each other and said,

"Yeah, we need to do something for that man outside." We went to the food section, purchased a few items, and took them outside to give to the man—this stranger, our neighbor. We didn't want to make a big deal of it so as not to demean him. We just handed him the items and said, "God bless you, brother," as we kept walking.

He replied, "Thank you and God bless you." I could not help but wonder how many strangers we followers of Christ encounter without stopping—even for just a minute or two—to offer help.

We read in Hebrews 13:2: "Do not forget to entertain strangers, for by so doing some people have entertained angels without knowing it." I hope you will think about this verse—and about Jesus' words in Matthew—the next time you encounter a stranger. When you extend a loving, helping hand, think about an angel in heaven singing, "Holy, holy, holy is the Lord God almighty." I don't know what heaven will be like, but I wonder if we will meet angels there who will say to us, "Thank you for helping me when I was a stranger." I *do* know that Jesus' account of the man who was beaten up and left on the side of the road ought to make us mindful of the strangers we encounter today and of our responsibility to show them compassion. For strangers though they may be, they are our neighbors.

11

My Neighbor Is Someone Who Has Been Stripped

The victim in the parable of the Good Samaritan was not just robbed and beaten. The Scripture text tells us that he was also stripped of his clothing. He was naked. In an earlier chapter we explored what it means to be naked, and how it feels to have other people know things about us that we prefer they not know—things that make us feel embarrassed and insecure.

At some point every day, we are all naked. When we take a bath or change clothes, we become naked. We ought not to find that embarrassing. Probably most people don't even give it much thought. But to be stripped is something entirely different. To be stripped is to be rendered naked by force, against our will. We hear from time to time of someone being strip-searched and those of us who haven't experienced that can only imagine how humiliating it must be.

Had those robbers taken all of this man's money and everything he was carrying, but left him his clothes, at least he would have been left with something, however little. But to be stripped is to have *everything* taken away, to be down to nothing. To be robbed and beaten and wounded is bad enough, but then to be stripped on top of that is like having salt rubbed into the wound.

To be stripped is not just about losing clothes. It is to be deprived of dignity—of one's personhood, one's humanity. This is a tragedy, because all human beings on the face of the earth have a rightful claim to dignity. To deny this claim is to insult and offend our heavenly Father, because we were all created in the image of God, and all of us bear His likeness.

Even those who are on the so-called bottom rung of the social ladder—people who have no money, no home to live in, no family or friends to look after them—still have as much right as anyone to claim dignity, because no matter what their state in life or what they have done, they were created in the image of God.

Sadly, we live in a society where both individuals and institutions seek to strip people by chipping away at their rightful claim to dignity. People are stripped of their dignity in many ways: through racial slurs, discriminatory housing practices, and a health care system that prevents them from getting the care they need, to name a few. Sometimes they are stripped at least partly as a result of their own shortcomings and mistakes. Such persons still have dignity. They are, like all of us, imperfect people. They are broken vessels. And they are our neighbors.

Do you know someone who has been stripped? Maybe someone who was stripped of their driver's license? Perhaps someone who was stripped of a job because of downsizing or maybe because they made some mistake? Is there someone you know who has lost his or her family? It's not for us to try to determine who is at fault and to assign blame. Our first step is to recognize that the person who has been stripped needs our help. Instead of being strippers of dignity, we need to be restorers of dignity. Because the person who has been stripped is our neighbor.

12

My Neighbor Is a Foreign Traveler

The man who was beaten up and left on the side of the road to die was apparently on a journey of some kind. We don't know for sure, but he was very likely a traveler in foreign territory, unfamiliar with the nooks and crannies along the path, the trees and rocks that robbers liked to hide behind. Had this traveler possessed inside information as to which places to avoid, he might not have been robbed in the first place.

We have many foreign travelers in our land today. We know them as immigrants, though some refer to these people as "illegal aliens." In fact, what to do about these foreign travelers has become a huge political issue in America today. A lot of people are afraid of these foreign travelers coming to our land, even though, except for Native Americans, pretty much everyone who lives in the U.S. descended from people who came here as foreign travelers, whether from Europe, Asia, Africa or somewhere else.

People who have lived here for a longer time are afraid that the newcomers will take away American jobs, even though by and large these foreign travelers are doing work most Americans don't want to do—work that in many instances helps businesses in our country remain viable. For example, 65 percent of dishwashers in America are of Mexican descent. It's a minimum (or below minimum) wage job—not something most Americans would choose.

I don't know that I've ever met anyone who, when asked what they aspired to do in life, said, "I want to be a dishwasher." Of course, there's nothing wrong with being a dishwasher, for there is dignity in *any* kind of work. Still, we can understand that many people aspire to do something more.

I recognize that immigration, as a political issue, is complex. I don't understand all of the legal ins and outs or the economic implications. But I do understand how we, as Christ's followers, are to treat immigrants: "When foreigners reside among you in your land, do not mistreat them" (Leviticus 19:33, *TNIV*). We cannot prevent the politicians and builders of walls and law enforcement officials from doing what they feel they need to do. But as Jesus' followers, we must not mistreat foreign travelers, and we must not judge them based on the country they came from or how well they speak English.

Leviticus 19:34 goes further: "The foreigners residing among you must be treated as your native-born" (*TNIV*). This means, for example, that we can't say, "They are taking our jobs away from us." We can't say this because *they* are *us*. These foreign travelers are our neighbors, and we are to love them as we love ourselves. And I believe that as we do that, other people will be able to tell that we love Jesus and want to walk in His steps as much as we can.

I remember an article in the *Chicago Tribune,* titled "A Foot in the Kitchen Door," about a young man named Pedro, who started working at a Lou Malnati's restaurant in the Lawndale community. Pedro was born in Mexico and came to the U.S. in 1986 at the age of 18. He started as a busboy, and then graduated to dishwasher. The article explored the struggles and hardships that come with being an immigrant, but the bottom line was that by 2006, Pedro had become a corporate executive at Lou Malnati's.

Foreign travelers in our country are routinely abused and mistreated because they are so desperate and have so few choices. But a wonderful man named Marc Malnati serves as a shining example of how we ought to be treating persons who arrive in our communities from faraway places.

The Malnati organization opened a restaurant in the Lawndale community in the mid-1990s to invest in our neighborhood and to provide a safe, smoke-free and friendly environment for families to go out to eat where previously none existed. Even today, the restaurant loses money, but the Malnatis continue to invest. I've observed how Marc Malnati deals with the immigration issue. Suffice it to say that Pedro's story is not an isolated one. Marc, a Christ follower, started English language classes, free of charge, for his workers, so that those who had come here from Mexico, though they might start off as a busboy or dishwasher, could go on to become servers or cooks or even, in time, executives. In other words, he treats foreign travelers as if they belong here as much as anyone.

If you have not already, I'm sure that sometime soon you will have the opportunity to reach out to a foreign traveler—someone who has come a long way and who feels alone and possibly afraid most of the time. These are people Christ calls us to love. They are our neighbors, whom we are to love as we love ourselves.

13

My Neighbor Has Been Beaten Up

It's not often that we run across someone who has been physically beaten. I am confident, however, that the overwhelming majority of people who follow Christ, if they encountered such a person, would stop, as the Good Samaritan did, to offer first aid or to call for medical assistance. I am more concerned about how often we stop to help those who have been beaten up in other ways.

Not long ago, I attended a high school basketball game. A boy on one of the teams made a mistake. Even though it was a very small mistake, it was enough to prompt his coach to call a timeout. It was a 30-second timeout, which means that the players aren't allowed to sit down. Instead of giving his team some encouragement or strategic advice, this coach spent at least 28 of his 30 seconds in the face of the boy who'd made the mistake, yelling at him the whole time.

During that 30-second timeout, the boy's entire demeanor changed. Up to that point, he had been bright-eyed, excited and energetic. He was having fun. Not long before the timeout, he'd hit a three-pointer, and he'd made a few others prior to that. He was grabbing some rebounds, hustling down the court, and all in all doing a lot of good things. His team was winning the game. But during those 30 seconds, the coach focused only on the one mistake this boy had made. And I watched as the look on his face went from almost joyful excitement to a sort of dismal defeat. The gleam in his eye disappeared. It was as if someone was pouring concrete on him. He slumped over, slouching his shoulders and dropping his head.

Everything in me wanted to run out onto that court, throw my arms around this kid, look him straight in the eye, and say, "Hold your head up, young man. You are a wonderful human being. You were created in the image of God. Your mom and dad love you. God loves you. We care about you! And no mistake you ever make on the basketball court, no matter how big, can change any of that even one little bit."

I didn't do what I wish I could have done. But it occurred to me that each day of my life, I encounter people who need someone to put his or her arms around them and say to them something along the lines of what I wanted to say to that high school basketball player. I'm thinking primarily about people who have been beaten not with fists, but by words. There's even a name for this: verbal abuse. Parents put down their children, husbands demean their wives and vice versa. Sometimes people are put down by their bosses or by others who are in positions of authority over them.

The verbal abuse might seem minor, but if it takes place consistently over time, it wears people down to a point where they feel weak and depressed—beaten up. It might take all the energy they have just to get up in the morning and go to work or to school. People who have been abused verbally know that the little playground rhyme, "Sticks and stones can break my bones, but words will never hurt me" is nonsense. Words *do* hurt. Words can break our hearts and drain us of our energy—our zest for life.

Jesus' vision for how we should treat others provides a stark contrast. In Luke 4, He quotes the prophet Isaiah: "The Spirit of the Sovereign Lord is on me, because the Lord has anointed me to proclaim good news to the poor. He has sent me to bind up the brokenhearted" (Isaiah 61:1, *TNIV*). Part of our job as Christ followers is to participate in Christ's mission to "bind up the brokenhearted."

As we seek to bind up the brokenhearted, we would do well to remember the message found in Colossians 3:12—that as God's chosen people, Christ's followers, we are "holy and dearly loved." As people who are dearly loved by God, we have the opportunity each day to clothe ourselves in the garments of "compassion, kindness, humility, gentleness and patience" in our interactions with other people.

I have been greatly influenced by the basic messages found in Tom Rath and Dr. Donald O. Clifton's book *How Full Is Your Bucket?* The book is based on the idea that everyone has a "bucket" that is empty, full or somewhere in between. The premise of the book is that every time we say or do something positive for another person, we help to fill his or her bucket. On the other hand, if we say or do something negative, we help to drain the person's bucket.

That's simple enough. But here's the profound part. When we do positive things for others, it's not only *their* buckets we fill, but our own as well. Conversely, when we are negative toward others, we drain not just their buckets, but our own as well. Every time we say or do something negative to another human being, it zaps that person of his or her energy—we empty our neighbor's bucket. And we empty our own buckets, too.

If you think about this, you'll realize that people who are constantly putting others down are people who don't feel good about themselves. When someone says something negative about another person, if that other person isn't around to hear it, it won't drain her bucket. But it will still drain the bucket of the negative person. That's why we can all attest to the fact that people who are constantly criticizing others are the least happy people we know and the hardest people to be around.

So my message to people is this: If you want to stop being miserable, start doing nice things for others and saying nice things to them. If you want to fill your bucket, be kind to every human being you see. Smile at them, be polite, be cheerful, spread the joy of the Lord, be sensitive to whatever struggles they might be facing, and offer help. If more people lived like this, all of our buckets would get filled.

Those who have been beaten up, however, don't have enough people around them filling their buckets. The messages they have received from others, often including those who are supposed to love them the most, are all negative. And they've learned to be negative in return, which, again, only empties their buckets even more. It's like a downward spiral for people who have been drained over and over again.

According to Rath and Clifton, each moment of every day we have the opportunity to make choices to help fill or help empty other people's buckets. How we respond will have a profound influence not just on others, but on our own relationships, our own productivity, our own health, and our own happiness.

The challenge for Christ followers is to be different from the world. The challenge is to choose to be around those persons whom nobody wants to be around—people whose buckets are so drained, so empty, that they've lost hope of things ever being any different than they are right now.

Our neighbors are people who have been beaten up, perhaps by a basketball coach, or a parent or spouse, or a co-worker or boss, or maybe by all of the above and more. Every negative message— "you're no good," "you're a failure," "nobody cares about you"— has taken a toll. Those who have had their buckets drained need people to come around and fill their buckets up instead of ignoring them because they are hard to be around. I hope you will be one of those bucket-filling persons.

Who is my neighbor? It's that person who has been beaten up. Jesus taught us to love those persons, no matter how unlovable their injuries have caused them to be.

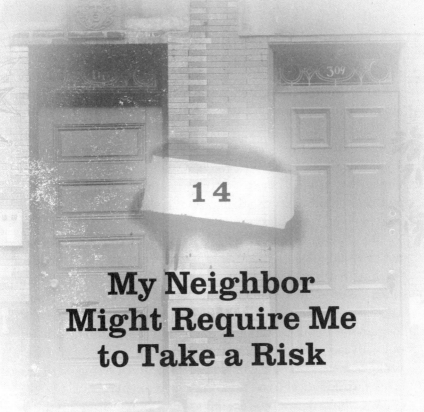

14

My Neighbor Might Require Me to Take a Risk

Each day of our lives we make decisions—some of them minor, some of them major—about what to do and what not to do. Especially with the tough decisions, it's common to weigh the "pros" against the "cons." In so doing, we examine both the certain and the potential gains of each path that lies before us. We set these alongside the definite and possible losses. In other words, we consider both the risks and the likely or potential rewards.

Successful businesses routinely conduct this kind of risk/reward analysis. If a particular venture is high-risk/low-reward, it's a "no-brainer." Why take a big risk for a small reward? The same is true of low-risk/high-reward scenarios. Why not take a small risk if the potential for a great reward is high? The toughest decisions are those in which both the potential for gain and the potential for loss are high.

Had the Good Samaritan conducted a risk/reward analysis before stopping to help the man who'd been beaten up and left on the side of the road, he likely would have concluded that helping the man was a high-risk/low-reward venture and thus was not worth it. To put it another way, he had a lot to lose and little, if anything, to gain, at least from a human standpoint.

When the Levite and the priest conducted their risk/reward analyses, each of them decided not to get involved. They knew that it was a dangerous area. Whoever had robbed and beaten the man might do it again. They stood to lose some of their possessions, and they could have lost their lives. So they played it safe and walked on by.

But if we are to love our neighbors as Jesus wants us to, we cannot be afraid to take risks. There are many things we stand to lose when we reach out to help other persons. We risk losing money when we try to help someone financially, especially if we don't know if the person is responsible or trustworthy. We might risk losing some of our power or damaging our reputation if we hang out with the "wrong kind of people"—drug dealers or ex-convicts or the homeless or those who don't look or smell very good. After all, the world judges us by the company we keep.

We would do well to remember that, along with everything else He was when He walked the earth, Jesus was a big-time risk-taker. The very act of coming to earth to live among us was a risk. We read in Philippians 2 that Christ did not count equality with God as something to be grasped. So He risked all He had in heaven and remained obedient to the Father "even to death on a cross."

The Gospels are full of accounts of Jesus taking risks. In Matthew 12, we find Him being confronted by the religious leaders of the day, who were testing Him on the question of whether healing on the Sabbath violated the command to keep the Sabbath holy. Dozens of man-made laws had been developed—laws that conflicted with the essence of a gospel of love. Right in front of all those people who were convinced it was wrong to heal on the Sabbath, Jesus took the risk of approaching a man in need of healing and said, "Stretch out your hand." And after Jesus healed the man, we read in verse 14, the religious leaders of the day "went out and plotted how they might kill him."

Jesus risked His reputation by hanging out with prostitutes. He also socialized with tax collectors, who were among the most despised people of Jesus' day, often because they regularly kept way more than their fair share of what was supposed to go to Rome. In Luke 19, we read about Zacchaeus, who was not just a tax collector but a chief tax collector. As we know, Zacchaeus took a risk of his own just by going out in public. When he quite literally went out on a limb, Jesus took the risk of inviting Himself to Zacchaeus's house for dinner. This action did not go unnoticed: "The people saw this and began to mutter" (Luke 19:7). Jesus was a risk-taker.

I am not suggesting that people should go about haphazardly taking unwise and unnecessary risks for no good reason. We need to wear seatbelts; we shouldn't be talking on cell phones while driving; we should look out for our own physical safety. But within this context, there are times when Christ followers need to take a risk—a step of faith.

Several years ago, before our church established Hope House for men trying to become productive members of society, a man who'd just gotten out of prison came to the church looking for help. He was on the verge of homelessness and needed a job. We didn't have a job to offer him, but we asked if he'd be willing to come by the church from time to time to volunteer, which is a good way for a person to show other people that he or she is reliable and trustworthy.

This man took us up on our offer and did a great job. We came to recognize that he had some construction skills, so we started paying him to do small construction projects. He was so reliable and such a hard worker that we referred him to a jobs program. He went through a three-month probationary period working for a big company in Chicago, and there were no problems. He always showed up on time and did his work well. But when it came time to hire him permanently, the company did a background check, which revealed that he'd been to prison. I still remember how deflated he was when they turned him away.

We have at our church a program called Jobs for Life that helps people find employment. We include "ex-offenders" because we believe that people ought to have another chance to show that they can be trusted. A Christian company about an hour's drive away informed us that they would hire people who completed our Jobs for Life program, even if these people had a criminal record or had struggled with a drug problem in the past.

The owner of the company even bought the church a minivan and pays all the expenses to transport people back and forth to work. A couple of dozen people from our church got jobs with this company. The opportunity has succeeded in giving some people a brand new start. It hasn't worked for everyone. Some lost their jobs because they were unreliable. A couple of men relapsed into a drug habit. Sometimes things don't work out the way we want them to. That's why it's called a risk.

To love our neighbors as Jesus would have us love them entails taking risks. And we can't stop taking risks the first time something goes wrong. Christ followers seek not to be safe, but to be faithful. The Good Samaritan stopped to help despite the risk that he might get beaten up himself. Who is my neighbor? It's that person for whom a risk might be required.

15

My Neighbor Can't Walk

When the Good Samaritan discovered the man who'd been beaten and left to die, one of the things he did for him was to take care of his wounds. He bandaged them and poured oil and wine on them. Then he put the man on his own donkey so he could get him to an inn. We can safely conclude that the man who'd been beaten was unable to walk. Maybe he had a broken leg; perhaps both his legs were broken. Maybe he was unconscious. Whatever the reason, he could not walk.

Our neighbors are people who are unable to walk. Chances are you know someone who works with you or attends your church or lives near you who is unable to walk—someone who has what today we call a "disability." Many such persons need a wheelchair to get from place to place. Sometimes they can get around on their own; sometimes they need another person's help.

Jesus regularly worked with people who had one kind of disability or another. In Matthew 15:30, we read: "Great crowds came to Him, bringing the lame, the blind, the crippled, the mute and many others, and laid them at his feet; and he healed them." Jesus clearly had great concern and compassion for people who were not physically whole. I suspect He had this concern partly because the physical is so intertwined with the emotional and the spiritual.

In Jesus' time, disabled persons were at a great disadvantage when it came to earning a living, enjoying the pleasures of life, and fulfilling the dreams they might have had. The same is true today.

We have a disabled person in our church, Keith, who is confined to a wheelchair as a result of muscular dystrophy. He can't build strength; the most he can do is work to try to maintain the strength he has.

Once, during a sermon on this topic, I invited Keith to come forward and tell the congregation a little bit about what life is like for him and what he expects and hopes for from others. Keith shared that he just wants to be considered a regular person, though for a long time he considered himself to be "irregular." As a younger person, he regarded himself almost as an alien. Now that he's older, he doesn't think that way anymore.

Keith recalled an occasion when he was being pushed down the street, and someone who was driving by rolled down the car window and screamed things like "cripple" and "retard." He talked about being in a store when a child noticed him and called his mother over, saying, "Look, Mama, look." This childlike innocence didn't bother Keith at all. What hurt him was when the mother grabbed and scolded the child. Keith said he made brief eye contact with the mother, but she quickly turned away like he wasn't even there, or as if he had some kind of contagious disease.

Keith went on to say that all he wants is for people to recognize that he is human, just like everyone else. He doesn't mind when curious children see him in a wheelchair and find it interesting. That's better than running away. He understands that people will stare at him, but he wants them not just to stare, but to speak to him, too.

Keith talked also about how difficult it is for him to accept the help that he sometimes needs. He wants to be independent and self-sufficient, yet he has to humble himself sometimes and allow others to pick him up and carry him somewhere. But he doesn't like it when people don't allow him to do what he can for himself—when they just jump in without asking if he would like some help.

Keith's experiences and insights ought to make us more sensitive to the needs and the feelings of disabled persons with whom we interact from time to time or perhaps on a regular basis—those who are blind or who have trouble walking or are confined to a wheelchair. These people are our neighbors. They don't want us to feel awkward around them, nor do they want us to assume that they always need or want our help.

Disabled persons simply want to be treated with the same dignity and respect we ought to afford all human beings. Unfortunately, too many people, not knowing what to do or say, simply ignore them. The next time you encounter someone with a disability, remember that he or she is your neighbor. And Jesus calls us to love our neighbors.

16

My Neighbor Looks Horrible

When I picture in my mind the person who was beaten and left on the side of the road, I see someone who is, to say the very least, not a pretty sight. In fact, he most certainly looks horrible. He's probably bleeding; his face is bruised and swollen. Most likely he looks like a boxer after a 15-round fight—fat lips, bloody nose, and eyes swollen shut. I regret to say that I've seen people shortly after they've been severely beaten. And, quite frankly, I found it nauseating.

Seeing someone who has been beaten can also be a scary thing. Perhaps it's because we think about the possibility that the same thing can happen to us. Or maybe it's because the person's face is so distorted that it reminds us of some monster in a horror film. Whatever the reason, seeing someone who's been beaten makes us fearful.

Who are the people in our world today who look horrible—who look a little scary? One group that comes to mind is the homeless—people who, through a combination of things that have happened to them and choices they've made, have landed on the street. They are not easy to look at. They are usually dirty and smelly. Their clothes are out of style and don't fit. Their hair is greasy and uncombed. The cardboard boxes they use to shield themselves from the elements are not exactly a realtor's dream. Suffice it to say it's not pretty.

It's hard to look at a person who seems to have no purpose or goal in life, no plan, and no initiative. We see that little cup they put out there to collect some money, and people who care naturally want to put something in. That's not the way to love our neighbor. Rather, what those persons who are destitute need is for others to follow the example of the Good Samaritan. They need someone who will do more than throw a dime or dollar into a cup. They need someone who will get involved in their lives—who will get personal.

The Samaritan approached the horrible-looking man, bandaged his wounds, picked him up, put him on his donkey, and then took him to an inn. Can you imagine the time it took for him to do all that? But he took the time and made the effort to get personally involved, realizing that the man on the side of the road needed far more than spare change.

We, too, need to get personally involved in the lives of our neighbors. That's how we demonstrate love. We engage our horrible-looking neighbors in conversation. We find out what they need. And we make sure we're prepared to direct them to food cupboards and shelters and job training programs and other resources that can help them turn their lives around.

We have challenged the people at our church to invite homeless men to Hope House, to pay for their train rides to get there, and perhaps even to stop for some food on the way. Because I believe that truly loving our neighbors in this case means helping them get to a place where they don't have to sit on a street corner and beg. But first, we put them on our donkeys and take them to an inn.

It's not just homeless persons who live nearby who look terrible. It's also children overseas whose bellies are bloated because they have nothing to eat. Even though they live far away, these children, who are too powerless to fend for themselves, are our neighbors. We can't go on thinking that there is nothing we can do to alleviate poverty in other parts of the world. That's a cop-out. There are many worthy organizations, including Christian organizations, that are working to bring an end to the hunger pangs of our neighbors who live far away. They need our help, and when we provide that help, we are loving our neighbors as Jesus would have us love them.

We are instructed to welcome horrible-looking people into our fellowship. The second chapter of James talks about two people who come to church, that is, to the synagogue. One of them is all decked out in fine clothes and jewelry. The other is poor and wearing old, filthy clothes and is probably smelly. James says, basically, in verses three and four: "If you show special attention to the one wearing fine clothes and say, 'Ah, here's a good seat for you; come on up here and sit at the front,' but then you say to the poor, 'You stand there; you stand over there in the corner. You can't even come all the way in.' Or, 'You come sit at the feet, but you don't get a chair,' then, 'Have you not discriminated among yourselves and become judges with evil thoughts?'"

For the record, Lawndale Community Church is my favorite church in America. My second favorite church is one that meets under a bridge in Waco, Texas. In fact, the church is called the Church Under the Bridge. Janet and Jimmy Dorrell, along with a few other people, started this church because homeless people were sleeping under the bridge, and no church would let these homeless people into their building on Sunday.

They have some interesting characters at the Church Under the Bridge, including one guy who's both physically impaired and mentally challenged. In fact, he's probably schizophrenic, but he has no access to medication. He loves music, even though he doesn't know the first thing about playing it. So they give him a guitar, but they don't plug it in. And when their praise team is up there leading worship, he's up there, too, playing and singing. It might be the only hour of the week when this man feels happiness.

I've had the privilege of preaching four or five times at the Church Under the Bridge. It's definitely a different kind of experience, in part because you wonder if anybody's hearing a word you're saying. The times I've preached there, people have been walking all around. Cars scream by on Interstate Highway 35. The bridge shakes when semi-trucks cross it. When the wind kicks up, it turns the pages of open Bibles. People in the congregation smoke cigarettes. Once, a guy approached me in the middle of my sermon to offer me a mint.

On one occasion, I asked one of the men there to tell me about his experience. He pointed to a church whose steeple was visible just a few blocks away. And he said, "I grew up going to church. I wanted to go to church. And I went over there, and the ushers and the deacons stopped me and told me I couldn't come in." This church didn't even do what James warns us about. They didn't let this man sit on the floor or stand in the corner.

But now this same man is one of the leaders of the Church Under the Bridge. It's a congregation of people who are smelly, whose clothes are tattered and torn, and whose hair is a mess. They really do look terrible. But Janet and Jimmy and others in Waco have come alongside them and have turned this space under the bridge into a wonderful, sacred space.

One time, I slept on the old gravel under the bridge with some of the homeless people and with Pastor Jimmy. It wasn't easy. In fact, afterwards I was sick for a week. But I have no regrets because I think we need to take opportunities, from time to time, to identify with homeless persons and others who may look horrible to us.

Who do you see that, based on how they look, might cause you to turn the other way instead of stopping? Jesus calls us to demonstrate our love by stopping to help—by getting involved. These people may look horrible. But they are our neighbors, and we are called to view them through the eyes of love.

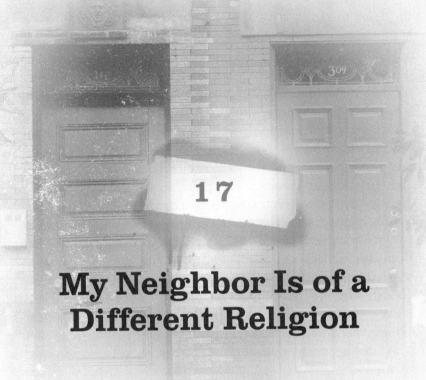

17

My Neighbor Is of a Different Religion

Fifty years or so ago, very few people in the U.S. lived near someone who practiced a religion different from theirs. Times have changed. Today, our society is not just multicultural, but it is multi-religious, too. It's not uncommon for us to encounter Muslims and Hindus, as well as groups such as Jehovah's Witnesses, Mormons and other sects that have strayed from Christian orthodoxy.

The person who was beaten and left on the side of the road was a Jew. The man who stopped to help him, as we know, was a Samaritan. Earlier we discussed the ethnic differences between Samaritans and Jews. (The Samaritans were of mixed race.) But in addition to the ethnic differences, there was also a religious difference.

Samaritans, in essence, had taken certain Old Testament Scriptures and reinterpreted them in their own way. Thus, it's likely that the way that Jews in Jesus' time regarded Samaritans is something akin to how Christians today might regard a cult or unorthodox religious sect. Suffice it to say that Jews and Samaritans did not get along.

Typically, when we meet people from other religions, we harbor feelings of distrust. We tend to dislike people of other religions. Sometimes we fear them. Many in America, after the horror of 9-11, began looking at all Muslims as the enemy, even though the terrorist attacks were the actions of a very small number of extremists.

It should go without saying that we should not consider people enemies simply because they practice another religion. But Jesus makes it very clear, in the Sermon on the Mount, that even if we do consider other people our enemies, it is still our responsibility to love them. He is recorded in Matthew 5:43-44 as saying, "You have heard that it was said, 'Love your neighbor and hate your enemy.' But I tell you: Love your enemies and pray for those who persecute you." He goes on to say, in verse 46, "If you love those who love you, what reward will you get? Are not even the tax collectors doing that?" So as Christians, we do not have the luxury of simply labeling someone our enemy so we don't have to be concerned with loving them.

I am of the mind that if we are confident in the truth of our Christian faith, we have no reason to dislike or fear people of other religions. Unfortunately, sometimes Christians fear people of other faiths because, on some level, they feel threatened. They're not sure that their faith in Christ and devotion to Christianity can hold up to Islam or some other religion.

As we look to Jesus as our model, we see that He had no fear of interacting with people of different religions. We read in John 4 that Jesus decided to go from Judea to Galilee after He learned that the Pharisees had heard He was gaining and baptizing more disciples than John. To get to Galilee, He went through Samaria—through this place that was home to a different religion, and to people whom many Jews considered the enemy.

What's more, Jesus apparently had no reservations when it came to interacting with Samaritans and engaging them in conversation. We read that, after sending His disciples off for food, He sat down by the well of Jacob. He was thirsty. A Samaritan woman came to the well, and Jesus said to her, "Will you give me a drink?"

It's hard for us today to fully understand how astonishingly radical a thing this was for Jesus to do. First, in that culture, a Jewish man would never lower himself by speaking publicly to any woman, let alone a Samaritan woman. The Samaritan woman realizes instantly that Jesus' action is, to say the least, out of the ordinary. She says to Him, "You are a Jew and I am a Samaritan woman. How can you ask me for a drink?" The gospel writer adds the parenthetical observation, "For Jews do not associate with Samaritans."

Jesus goes on to reach out to this woman spiritually. He offers her living water, the kind that leads to eternal life. He then tells the woman to go home and bring back her husband so He can have a conversation with him, too. When she says, "I have no husband," Jesus tells her that He knows she has had five husbands. The woman realizes that Jesus is a prophet, and her life is changed. We read later in John 4 that many Samaritans came to believe in Jesus because of this woman's testimony.

In this passage, Jesus demonstrates for us that we need not be afraid of somebody of a different religion. In fact, we can enter into dialogue and actually have a relationship with such a person. In his book *Just Walk Across the Room,* Willow Creek Community Church pastor Bill Hybels tells the story of how he came upon that book's title. At a Christian gathering, he had met an African-American man with a Muslim-sounding name. Pastor Hybels engaged the man in conversation. The man told him that he used to be Muslim. He went to a business meeting, and someone he'd never met, a man who was a Christian, walked across the room to introduce himself.

The Christian man said he knew very little about Islam, and he asked this Muslim person he'd just met to tutor him. So the two started getting together on Saturday mornings to read the Koran, and so the Muslim man could tell his new friend what Muslims believe.

After about six weeks, the Muslim man asked his Christian friend to teach him more about Christianity. So for the next few Saturdays, they got together to read the Bible and talk about

Christianity and what it means to be a follower of Christ. As a result, the Muslim man became a Christian. It happened because someone left his comfort zone, walked across the room, and was not afraid to enter into a dialogue with someone from another religion.

We need not be afraid of people of other faiths. In fact, as Jesus demonstrated, we are to love those persons because they are our neighbors. This love can begin by forming a relationship with these persons. That's what Jesus did. He didn't just talk to the woman at the well; He also listened.

At least a couple of mornings each week, I have breakfast at Manny's, a Jewish deli. I started going there mainly because it opens at five in the morning. I go there almost every Saturday morning at five, and I spend the next three or four hours finishing my sermon. I have my own little table, and nobody bothers me. The servers bring me all the coffee I want.

Often, during the week, there's a Jewish man, Ron, who sits right next to me. Ron grew up in Lawndale, so naturally we have an ongoing dialogue. I've been getting to know him. I prayed for his mother when she was sick. And I prayed for him when his mother passed away. I've asked for his thoughts on topics from the Old Testament, since he goes to the synagogue faithfully every week. He's also told me things about what it was like to grow up in Lawndale and often gives me history lessons concerning various places in our community.

I've also had some good conversations with Ken, the owner of this Jewish deli. Once I wrote out a little list—David Letterman style—of the top 10 things I like about his place. I gave it to him and thanked him for running a business that helps me to be who I am. I've also spoken with Ken about President Barack Obama, who has been to Manny's many times. When he learned that President Obama had once attended Rick Warren's church in California, I told him about Warren's bestselling book *The Purpose-Driven Life*. When he expressed interest in the book, I got a copy for him.

When Anne and I went to Israel, I picked up rocks from the stream where David got his five smooth stones to kill Goliath. I gave one to Ron and one to Ken, and I read them the passage in

1 Samuel 17. We all carry the small stones in our pockets, and this continues to be an encouragement to each of us when we face the giants in our lives.

I don't have any agenda for these conversations other than just getting to know each other. But I'm glad to be involved in them, because I believe that's what Jesus would do. We ought not to be afraid of people of other faiths, whether they are Buddhist, Hindu, Mormon, Jehovah's Witness or Muslim. In fact, they are our neighbors, and we are called to love our neighbors.

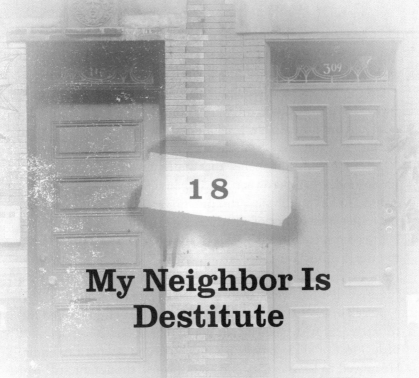

18

My Neighbor Is Destitute

The man who was beaten up and left to die on the side of the road was destitute. To be destitute means essentially that you've got nothing left. You're out of options—no food, clothing or shelter, and no means of subsistence. Everything's been taken away. That was the condition of this man on the side of the road.

I'd like to share a story of someone who knew firsthand what it was like to be destitute—someone who, after escaping his condition, went on to model for us how to reach out in love to those who are destitute. It's the true story of a man who grew up in Mississippi. This man had it pretty rough. His father was never around, never sent him a birthday card or a Christmas gift. In fact, he hardly ever saw his father.

His mother gave him away because she didn't want to raise him. So he lived with his grandparents. Not experiencing love from his parents affected this young man, as it would most people. When he finished high school, he went off to try to get his life together, but he went from job to job, unable to hold one down. After getting fired from a job in 1971, he ran out of money.

One morning, when he had not eaten for several days, he was so hungry that he walked into a place called the Dixie Diner, located somewhere in Mississippi. It's one of those diners where the owner is also the cook, the waiter, and the checkout clerk. Our man had been there a few times before. He went in with a plan to eat his food and then leave when the owner had his back turned.

But something happened that day that would turn this man's life around. When the owner gave him his bill, he was looking right at him, so he couldn't just run out. So he lied by saying he'd lost his wallet. The owner of the diner saw through the lie and had compassion. He looked at this destitute man and said, "Wait a minute, I think you dropped something." Then he stepped out from behind the counter, knelt down, and stood up holding a twenty-dollar bill, which he proceeded to give to the man.

Back in 1971, this was enough money to pay for his meal and fill up his car with gas. The gift got him back on his feet, if only a little. Most of all, it gave him some hope and strength to go on. He moved to Kansas City and found work, though he still had trouble keeping a job. In 1979, two weeks before Christmas, he got fired from a job he'd held for almost a year. He drove into one of those little drive-in, 1950s-style hamburger places and ordered a burger and a Coke.

He noticed that the woman who waited on him was wearing old clothes and a coat too thin and worn to keep her warm. He considered the possibility that her situation in life was worse than his. He had a $20 bill in his pocket, and he remembered the time the man in the diner had reached out to him. So he gave the woman the twenty and told her to keep the change.

The young woman's face exploded in a smile, which gave this man a whole new perspective on what is important in life. He prayed to God, feeling moved to help other people. He had about $600 in the bank. Even though he had no job, he withdrew some of his money and began looking for people who were worse off than he was so he could give his money away. He gave away a couple hundred dollars, 20 at a time, and almost instantly things began to improve for him.

He went on to find work and eventually started his own business. Every Christmas, like Scrooge after his transformation, he sought out people to give away money to. First it was $20 bills, but he eventually moved on to hundreds. When Oprah heard about this man's generosity, she had him on her show as a guest, but he wanted to remain anonymous, so he went only by the name "Secret Santa." Unfortunately, one of those tabloid newspapers that couldn't let a good thing go unveiled his identity: Larry Stewart.

A few years ago, Larry contracted throat cancer. Shortly before he passed away, he came to Chicago at Christmas time to give away money to families in need. He came to our church, and I was so glad for the opportunity to talk with him. A few families from Lawndale met us there, and he was able to give them a little bit of money to help them along.

Larry found a deep joy in helping other people. I believe that those who have experienced destitution, as Larry did, feel a special kind of joy when they reach out to others in need. But it's a joy that is open for all of us to experience.

America is a wealthy nation. But it is not hard to find people in our society who are destitute. And it's not only in big cities. Regardless of the reasons they are destitute, they are our neighbors, and they need our love. And when we love them, as Larry Stewart did, we will experience a special kind of joy.

19

My Neighbor Is a Victim of Injustice

We read in Luke 4 that when Jesus goes to the synagogue, He's asked to read from the Scriptures. He's given the scroll of Isaiah, and He can read anything He wants. He turns to chapter 61 and begins, "The Spirit of the Sovereign Lord is on me, because the Lord has anointed me to proclaim good news to the poor. He has sent me to bind up the brokenhearted, to proclaim freedom for the captives and release from darkness for the prisoners" (Isaiah 61:1, *TNIV*). The passage Jesus chose to read culminates in this declaration: "For I, the Lord, love justice; I hate robbery and wrongdoing" (Isaiah 61:8, *TNIV*).

One of my favorite Old Testament passages, Micah 6:8, advances a similar theme: "And what does the Lord require of you? To act justly and to love mercy and to walk humbly with your God."

The man who was beaten and left on the road to die was a victim of injustice. As Christ followers, we are called to stand with and walk alongside those who have been wronged.

Especially since I live and minister in a community made up mostly of African-American people, it is hard for me to think about injustice in our country without thinking about our history of slavery. The images of human beings chained in close quarters with no bathroom—having to sleep in their own vomit if they got sick—are hard to face, as is the knowledge that on many of these cross-ocean journeys, most of those who had been taken to be slaves died and were thrown to the sharks.

It didn't get much fanfare, but February 23, 2007, marked the 200th anniversary of the British Parliament's vote to abolish the slave trade. I am fascinated by the story of how the slave trade came to an end. William Wilberforce, because he was a member of Parliament, is the person most often associated with the abolition of British slave trading. But in fact, there was a whole team of people who contributed.

One of those people was an African from Nigeria named Equiano, who was stolen from his native land and taken to Jamaica as a slave. Equiano wrote a book, *The Interesting Narrative of the Life of Olaudah Equiano, the African*. It was published in 1789, and some 50,000 copies of it sold fairly quickly, which was really quite amazing for that time or any time. When Wilberforce found out about the book, he and Equiano became friends. Wilberforce regularly quoted Equiano's book in his speeches to Parliament.

Promotional materials for the 2007 movie *Amazing Grace* featured three people: Wilberforce, Equiano and John Newton, who is another person God used to bring an end to the trans-Atlantic slave trade. Newton, as the captain of a slave ship, had made numerous voyages from Africa to the Americas. Later in his life, he regularly suffered from nightmares as a result of the evil in which he'd participated. It was, of course, Newton who wrote the hymn "Amazing Grace" and the words "Amazing grace, how sweet the sound that saved a wretch like me." Most of us, when we sing this word "wretch," tend to think, "I'm not that bad." But it's not hard to understand why Newton considered himself a wretch.

One of the things that most amazes me about the story of the abolition of the slave trade is that it took so long. Wilberforce, who'd committed his life to Jesus Christ in 1785, made a commitment in 1787 to bring an end to British slave trading. It took 20 years for the mission to be accomplished. He made his first speech to Parliament on this topic in 1789. In the beginning, he was laughed out of Parliament because of the financial ramifications of abolishing the slave trade. But he did not give up.

Neither can we give up, though we may grow weary when progress seems slow or nonexistent. Loving our neighbors means speaking and working on behalf of victims of injustice—especially when those victims have no voice—even in the absence of clear results.

We do not have to search hard to find injustice. We still have an estimated 27 million slaves around the world today—people who have been taken away from their homes and forced to become prostitutes or to work against their will. We have nearly one million babies aborted in America every year. Although the trans-Atlantic slave trade is no more, racism still runs rampant around the world. In Africa, it comes in the form of tribalism. Here in America, we see it in policies and social conventions that unfairly keep people from getting a quality education or a decent house in which to live. People are discriminated against for many reasons—their gender, their skin color, and in some cases their physical size or beauty, as defined by the world.

We in the church need to take to heart the words found in Amos 5, where the prophet says in essence, "I can't stand your choir. I can't stand your music. I'm sick of the money you put into the offering. Because you're doing it at the same time you forget about justice." We read in verse 24: "But let justice roll on like a river, and righteousness like a never-failing stream!"

People in our world who have been wronged—who are victims of injustice—are our neighbors, and we are called to love them.

2 0

My Neighbor Has Been Passed By

To be passed over or passed by is to be ignored, considered insignificant, dehumanized. This was no doubt among the feelings experienced by the man who was beaten up and left to die on the side of the road. It was not by accident that he was passed over. Those who passed him by—first the priest and then the Levite—made a conscious choice to ignore someone who was in desperate need of help. Both were religious leaders—people who, at least in theory, were known for their spirituality and for serving God. Perhaps this was Jesus' way of saying that genuine spirituality is defined not by stature or position or title, but rather by how we love others.

Our neighbors are people who have in some way been passed over. People who live in inner cities know what it means to be passed over. Typically interstate highways have been built to bypass cities so people can get to where they want to go quickly and without having to risk encountering anyone who's been beaten up and might need a little help. Lawndale Community Church is located on Ogden Avenue, which was named for the first mayor of Chicago. Ogden Avenue, built in the mid-1800s, was in some ways a precursor to interstate highways. The mayor had this road built so there would be a quick way for him to get to his mill in the Western suburbs and bypass hurting people in the process.

Sometimes I wonder if the Jericho Road, like our modern-day interstate highways, was built specifically so people could get from Jerusalem to Jericho quickly and with minimal likelihood of encountering anyone from the lower echelons of society. Nowadays we might say the road was very commuter-friendly, but not very community-friendly.

People get passed over all the time. In fact, entire neighborhoods and communities get passed over. When I moved to Lawndale in 1975, I had to learn to live without a McDonald's Big Mac, because, as ever-present as this fast-food restaurant chain was in our country (and of course still is), there was no McDonald's in Lawndale until 1992. In terms of national chains, that's about all we have even today in Lawndale. The Red Lobsters and IHOPs and Olive Gardens of the world have pretty much all passed us by.

Most people know what it feels like to be passed by. Chances are you have been passed over for a job you really wanted. Your résumé was strong, and the interview went well. You did all the things you were supposed to do, but for whatever reason you got passed by. Perhaps you were in line for a promotion you felt you deserved, but it went to someone else. I've witnessed many a young person getting passed by during a sports contest. Knowing the way the system works, they jockey for position, sitting as close to the coach as possible so that when it's time to send in a sub, they'll be first in line. But then the system fails them, and they get passed over for someone else.

Getting passed over is a part of life. We all face disappointments, usually minor ones, pretty much every day. This should not make us feel jaded toward those who get passed over in ways that truly hurt.

I can still recall a major tragedy on the North Side of Chicago in which six children died in a house fire. We later learned that this family had no electricity and hadn't for quite some time—months in fact. They lit candles so they could have some light at night, and one of those candles apparently set the place on fire in the wee hours of the morning when the children were asleep.

There were all kinds of discussion and analysis about how this could have happened. Some blamed politicians; some blamed the electric company, the neighbors, or the school system. And probably all deserved some of the blame. The bottom line is that lots of people knew this family had no electricity, but nobody stepped up to help. This family got passed over.

Think about the people you encounter every day who get passed over—by their employers, by the health care system, and by other people. Think about the people you pass by who might need you to stop and help. Jesus is trying to teach us that our neighbors are people who get passed by. More than that, they get passed over by people who make it seem like it's acceptable to pass others by. What if you see someone who needs assistance, but you're the third person in line to help? The first person in line is a pastor, and the second is a deacon. You see both, instead of helping, crossing to the other side of the street and continuing on their way. This makes it seem okay for us to do the same. But it's not. Our mission is not to follow pastors or deacons, but to follow Jesus. Do you know someone who is hurting and gets passed by on a regular basis? That person is your neighbor.

21

My Neighbor Can't Say, "Thank You"

As we've seen, the man who was beaten and left to die was described as half dead. The Good Samaritan had a conversation with the innkeeper, but we have no record of any conversation with the man he was helping. Thus it's possible—even likely—that the man had been beaten so badly he was unable to speak. Perhaps he was unconscious, so that when he awoke in the inn he was unaware of what had happened to him and who had come to his aid. If this were indeed the case, he would have been unable even to say, "Thank you."

We all like to be thanked. We like to be recognized and appreciated for the good things we do. I've heard many a conversation in which someone talks about how he or she helped someone else and concludes, with frustration, "And he never even said, 'Thanks.'" I know I've said and thought that several times. It's almost as if we regret doing whatever we did to help the ungrateful person.

In Luke 17:17-18, we see that even Jesus, after healing 10 lepers, calls attention to the fact that only one of the 10 returned to thank Him. He asks, "Were not all ten cleansed? Where are the other nine? Was no one found to return and give praise to God except this foreigner?"

We can safely assume that the Good Samaritan did not expect to be thanked. Perhaps he figured he would never even be recognized for the good he had done. You might say that he acted anonymously. When we give anonymously, the recipient of our gifts has no way of thanking us.

Many have made the case that anonymous giving is the purest form of giving, because there can be no confusion or doubt about the motive. It's not the recognition or the thanks from others or the feeling of superiority that people who give anonymously seek. Rather, they give simply because it's a good thing to do, and perhaps so they can experience the pure joy that comes from helping another without expecting anything in return.

I'm not saying that giving anonymously is the only way to give. Nor am I saying that it's a horrible thing to be disappointed when people don't say, "Thank you." Certainly, we ought to express our gratitude when people help us, whether with a thank-you note or phone call or in some other way. But when we help somebody who is unable to thank us—either because he or she can't speak or because we have given anonymously—we are loving a neighbor.

We can help our neighbors anonymously in simple ways, perhaps by closing a gate that is open or picking up some trash that someone has thrown in their yard. Or by shoveling the sidewalks of elderly folks without leaving a note or telling them about it.

Our church has helped people anonymously in faraway places such as Ethiopia and Kenya, including children who will never be able to thank us. Our daughter, Angela, and I visited an orphanage in Kenya. The staff told us that people had supported them financially to supply Bibles and food, but they said they really needed a couple of bathrooms. No one wants to give money for a bathroom because it's not very glamorous. Our church did. The bathroom we sponsored isn't much to look at. It's just a 25-foot-deep hole in the ground and a building around it. When people use that bathroom at the orphanage, I doubt anyone is going to say thanks to us, but that doesn't and shouldn't matter. When we understand that the people we help are not able to thank us, our motivation changes. We do it totally for others and not for ourselves.

Perhaps you know how wonderful it feels to receive an anonymous gift. My wife, Anne, and I do. At one point, we were struggling financially, and out of nowhere came an anonymous gift of enough money to take care of our need. This was a real "God thing," because we hadn't told anybody about our struggles. We didn't know whom to thank, but that certainly didn't mean we weren't grateful.

As good as it feels to be on the receiving end of an anonymous gift, I challenge people to get to know what it feels like to be on the giving end. Who can you help who doesn't have the opportunity or the ability to thank you? It might be someone who lives close by or someone who is halfway across the world. Jesus teaches us that such persons are our neighbors.

22

My Neighbor Is Someone Who Has Been Wounded

Obviously, the man who had been beaten up and left to die had been wounded. Among the things the Good Samaritan did was to bandage those wounds. I want to focus here not on physical wounds, but rather on spiritual and emotional wounds, whose presence may not be so obvious. I want to discuss the "wounded heart" referred to in Psalm 109:22.

When I think of the word "wound," I tend to think of deep-seated injuries that do not heal quickly or fully. I think of conditions that may never go away—things that people have to learn to live with, sometimes even after many years of prayer and counseling. After all, the things that injure us may come to an end, but their effects can linger on.

Some of the wounds we face in life are wounds we get as children. Young people are not mature enough to process the things that happen to them and to put them in proper perspective. It brings tears to my eyes when I see children being wounded by their parents, the very people who should love them most in this world. One time, Anne and I were taking a walk on a beautiful fall day when we crossed paths with a mother and her small child. I still vividly recall the mother screaming at her child in public, even though this child had done nothing beyond what normal, healthy, inquisitive children do. She demeaned her child with words and threats of beatings. If somebody had said to me the things this mother said to her three-year-old, it would have taken at least a week, and a lot of people coming by to tell me how wonderful I am, for me to recover. Anne and I were devastated by the experience. I fear that children can be wounded so deeply that perhaps they cannot be fully un-wounded.

I feel especially for children of incarcerated parents. How hard it must be—how humiliating—for a child when the conversation with friends turns to parents. That child has to either lie or tell his friends that his mom or dad is in prison. That child's spirit—his heart—is wounded.

The Angel Tree ministry our church participates in provides gifts each Christmas for the children of incarcerated people. For me as a pastor, the day we give out the gifts is one of the most rewarding days of the year. Each December, I think about what a privilege it is to be a pastor at a church in which the overwhelming majority of the congregation finds joy in reaching out to hurting people, in particular to wounded children.

The talk I give each year is my favorite, because I get to tell these young people how very, very special they are. And that they've got a mom or a dad who loves them even though they can't be with them this Christmas. I tell them that Stanley and Antoinette, our Angel Tree leaders, have been in touch with their parents, and that their parents wanted to be sure each of them got a gift because they love their children. Our prayer is that this message will help heal the wounds they have received, though I know it's not that simple.

One year, on the day we gave out gifts, a mother came late, but was still hoping to get some gifts for her children. Fortunately we had a few left. I pulled this woman's four-year-old son aside and put my arm around him. He sat on my knee for a minute, and I said to him, "Now, you know who this gift is from, don't you?"

He pointed over to one of the people at the gift table and replied, "From her."

I said, "Oh, no. We're just the people giving it to you, but we're giving it to you from somebody else. This gift is from your daddy." His face lit up in a way that just made my day, made my week, made my month, made my year. I hoped that for him to know that his gift was from Dad—not from that person behind the table—might begin the process of healing his wounded spirit.

We are surrounded by people whose hearts have been wounded—people who have lost their jobs, their homes, their families, their joy, their purpose in life, or their health. Anne and I, as I suspect most people do, know of someone whose spirit has been wounded by a frightening diagnosis. For us, it was our friend Karen, when she was informed she had breast cancer. She fought through all the emotions and depression, and she endured the painful and draining treatments. Through medicine and God's healing power, she got through it. And today, her antennae go up immediately when she hears of another person associated with the words "breast cancer." She calls them on the phone, encourages them, and visits them in the hospital. In short, she does everything she can to redeem the woundedness she experienced. She does this by loving the neighbors who are experiencing wounds similar to hers.

This approach to loving others is modeled by the apostle Paul in 2 Corinthians 1, when he says, essentially, "I am struggling even to death, and I'm almost to the point of death, but it's happening for me so that I might help you" (see vv. 6,9). It is out of our own woundedness that we gain the ability to help other people.

Henri Nouwen shared Paul's understanding. His classic book *The Wounded Healer* features the discovery that it's out of our own woundedness that we have the ability to help others who have been wounded in the same or similar ways. According to Nouwen, the first thing we've got to do if we want to help others is admit that we are wounded ourselves. Then we need to go on from there to affirm that we don't have to be completely healed of our own wounds in order to help somebody else who has been wounded.

While accepting Jesus Christ as Savior and Lord gives us strength to endure and grow, it does not instantly take away our woundedness. It certainly didn't for the apostle Paul. But it's one thing to accept woundedness and live through it, and quite another thing to be so stuck in our own wounds that we never change and never reach out to help someone else who is in need.

According to Nouwen, if we're going to help another person, we need to get involved in the other person's life, as the Good Samaritan got involved in the life of the man who'd been beaten and left to die. By confessing our own woundedness, we are able to enter into the woundedness—the pain—of others.

No matter in which direction you look, each day you are sure to see many wounded people around you, though their wounds might not be readily obvious. Those wounded persons are your neighbors. Don't allow your own woundedness to keep you from acting. Instead, allow it to increase your capacity to understand and to love your neighbor as Jesus would have you do.

23

My Neighbor Is Someone Nobody Wants to Help

Because he was in a state of total helplessness, we can safely assume that the man who'd been beaten and left to die on the side of the road was hoping and praying that someone would come by. And we can assume also that he was praying for the *right* person to stop—someone who would come to his aid, not someone intent on exploiting him further, perhaps by finding out if he had anything left to steal.

Imagine how relieved the beaten man must have felt when he saw, of all people, a priest approaching. He must have thought that his prayers had been answered. Perhaps he was thinking that, for the rest of his earthly days, he would have this wonderful testimony about how, in a time of great vulnerability (to say the least), he prayed, and his prayers were answered almost instantly. But whatever joy he felt evaporated quickly when the priest simply moved to the other side of the road and walked right on by.

No doubt a Levite, another religious leader, was also high on the list of people the man was hoping would come by. In fact, maybe the Levite was in an even better position than the priest to stop and help. The priest may have been in a rush, on his way to carry out whatever priestly duties were on the docket for the day. But surely the Levite would stop. After all, isn't that what people of faith are *supposed* to do?

We can certainly understand why the man would be thinking this way. Imagine being in a position of total helplessness and vulnerability. Assuming you were even able to pray, you would most likely pray something like, "God, please send my pastor by to help me. If not the pastor, I'll settle for a deacon or an outreach counselor from the church. Or even a Sunday School teacher. I'll take anyone from the church."

A short time later, your pastor comes into view. Or a deacon from the church. And you shout, as loudly as you can, "Praise the Lord! Thank You, Jesus! My prayer's been answered." But then the person you were praying would come by makes a quick assessment of the situation and decides to move on, leaving you perplexed, disillusioned, and still in need of aid. This is exactly what the Levite did. He didn't want to get involved.

Our neighbors are those whom nobody, religious people included, wants to help.

Why do people, when they have the opportunity, decide not to stop to help other people? And, on a related note, why do some people get help while others don't? I have thought about this question a lot in the years following Hurricane Katrina, which, as we all know, devastated the Gulf Coast and New Orleans. Many times, I've looked at my own neighborhood of North Lawndale and imagined what it would be like to have every single building either wiped out or damaged so severely that it had to be torn down.

Several months after the Katrina disaster, violence erupted yet again in the Middle East. The group Hezbollah had set up headquarters in the country of Lebanon and started bombing Israel, which bombed back. The U.S. had a number of its citizens in

Lebanon at the time. No doubt they were, by and large, people of means, because it takes money to travel abroad.

I remember seeing footage of huge cruise ships, worth millions of dollars, sent by the U.S. to Lebanon to get our citizens out of the country and away from the danger. I could not help but contrast this image with the image of a rowboat going up and down the flooded streets of New Orleans in a desperate effort to rescue people from rooftops. Some of these people had to wait for several days for help to arrive.

My point here is that, with Katrina, there was some effort put forth to come to the aid of people in need. But it was far from the urgent, no-holds-barred, whatever-it-takes effort our country made to rescue its wealthy citizens from danger in Lebanon. Some people get help; others don't.

In Jesus' day, lepers were among those who could not count on any help from the government or from the society. In fact, lepers didn't even get to live in their area of choice. They were required to live with other lepers in colonies on the outskirts of town. According to the law, whenever lepers came into an area where there were other people around, they had to shout, "Leper! Leper! Unclean! Unclean!" One can only imagine the embarrassment associated with such a legal requirement.

The modern-day leper might well be the person who tests positive for the AIDS virus. Can you imagine somebody who is HIV-positive being required, upon coming through the church doors, to say, "HIV-positive! I've got AIDS! AIDS man or AIDS woman walking in!" Let's be honest, though, and admit that even though we don't ask people to shout it out, our society has its ways of keeping people with AIDS at a distance. There have been cases where doctors, nurses, schoolteachers and others have made it clear they don't want people with AIDS in their presence. Sometimes the discrimination is overt; more often than not, it is subtle.

Maybe the modern-day leper is the person on the street who's addicted to alcohol or who can't kick a drug habit. Maybe it's those who have been on and off drugs more times than they can count, so many times that people in a position to help have given up trying, that is, if they ever tried to help in the first place. Maybe it's a person known as an "ex-convict," someone who's just gotten out of prison. What if former inmates were required, upon walking into a room, to say, "Ex-con! Ex-con! I've been to prison!" Again, we don't require this, but we nevertheless treat them differently. Even though these people have paid their debts to society, most businesses won't give them jobs, and most people don't want them living in their neighborhoods.

Maybe it's the person with the bad reputation—someone who lives in the wrong part of town or hangs out with the wrong kind of people. We are tempted to ignore people like this and, if they need help, to look the other way.

Maybe the modern-day leper is that person who is just plain annoying. Most of us know someone like this—somebody who, every time you come into contact with him or her, gets on your last nerve. And this person gets on everyone else's last nerve, too, so you know it's not just you who feels that way.

Who will come to the aid of these people when the world has in some way beaten them up, cast them to the side of the road, and refused to help? I hope the answer to this question is you.

24

My Neighbor Is Lonely

The man who was beaten up and left to die on the side of the road was most likely traveling by himself. We don't know why. Perhaps he was a loner. Maybe someone was scheduled to take the trip with him but had to cancel at the last minute. In any case, traveling alone goes against common advice and conventional wisdom, both then and now.

It's always good to be with someone, or at least for another person to know where you are. Today, when children go on a school field trip or when scouts go on a camping expedition, they are routinely told, for reasons of safety, to abide by the "buddy system." That is, they are instructed to make sure they are always with one or more buddies. Safety comes in numbers.

In Jesus' time, as today, it was safer to travel in pairs. A robber would more likely attack someone walking alone than he would two people walking together. Perhaps this is one of the reasons Jesus sent His disciples out in pairs.

There are reasons beyond safety concerns to travel with another person. Human beings are meant to live in community. It's good to have someone to talk to and share problems with, especially if the journey is long. No one should have to go it alone. In other words: "Two are better than one, because they have a good return for their labor: If they fall down, they can help each other up" (Ecclesiastes 4:9-10, *TNIV*).

An extreme heat wave that hit Chicago in the summer of 1995 provided a vivid illustration of the consequences that can result from people being alone and lonely. On July 9 of that year, the thermometer hit 90 degrees. Temperatures climbed to 98 on July 12, then rose the next day to 106, the highest recorded temperature in Chicago's history. Things cooled down to highs of 102 on July 14, 99 the following day, and 94 on July 16 before finally dropping to 89 on July 17.

It wasn't much better at night, as lows remained in the high 70s or 80s. Chicago turned into what is known as an "urban heat island." Most of the city's buildings, because of the great Chicago Fire, were built with bricks and mortar. There's not much grass in the city of Chicago. All the bricks and mortar, along with all the concrete and asphalt streets, absorbed tremendous amounts of heat during the day and released little, if any, of this heat overnight. Apartments in the city became ovens.

What's more, during the week of this heat wave, there was almost no wind to cool things off even a little bit. So in addition to the heat, whatever pollution was in the air stayed right where it was, creating a sort of greenhouse effect—a cloud of heat and dead air over the city. Not a pretty picture.

Now, in a big city like Chicago, people die every day. But during the week of that 1995 heat wave, the death toll was 739 people above the normal rate for a week in the summer. In the midst of the heat wave, the coroner began to make estimates about the toll the heat would take on human lives. No one believed him at first, but the numbers didn't lie.

As people began to examine how it happened that so many people could perish during a heat wave, they found that the number one factor associated with dying from the heat was people, most of them elderly, living alone. Eric Klinenberg wrote a book about this titled *Heat Wave*, which he calls a social autopsy of this disaster. In 1999, the city experienced another heat wave, this one slightly less severe than the one before. By this time, people had stopped denying that heat presented a problem for people living alone. When it started getting hot, those in the news media took every opportunity to urge listeners to stay in touch with people who were alone—to call them or check in on them from time to time and make sure they had ways to stay cool or to get whatever help they needed to beat the heat. Though the number of heat-related deaths came down, still 125 died in the heat wave of '99.

The man who was beaten up and left on the side of the road was all alone. Our neighbors are, like this man, people who are alone. I'm sure we all know some of these people whom God loves. They might be physically alone, living by themselves with no one to talk with or to look out for them. Some are alone, and lonely, in different ways.

Maybe you know someone who is lonely as a result of a recent divorce, or someone who just lost his job, or someone struggling with illness in the family or who perhaps is ill herself. People facing these difficulties are prone to feel alone—abandoned by their friends and neighbors, and perhaps even by other family members. In their feelings of loneliness, they might perceive their situation to be worse than it is. In any case, they need a Good Samaritan—a good neighbor—in their lives. Let that good neighbor be you.

25

My Neighbor Will Cost Me Some Time

We can safely assume that the Samaritan who stopped to help the man who'd been beaten and left on the side of the road did not have a Day-Timer or Palm Pilot to help with his scheduling. Nevertheless, given his actions, we can reasonably speculate that he was a responsible person—someone who had a pretty full schedule, places to go and things to do. He was busy, but not too busy to stop and help someone who needed help.

Sometimes when we help others we just want to get it over with quickly: "Let's just do something fast, fix whatever the problem is, and move on. Give him a little pat on the back, put a Band-Aid on it, and tell him he can go now because everything is okay."

Well, everything might not be okay. Our neighbors are people who may require our time, including our "quality time" and sometimes more of it than we feel we are willing or able to give. The struggles, problems and life situations facing our neighbors more often than not require investments that go well beyond a few quick words of advice.

Who knows where the Samaritan was going or what he was on his way to do? He had a bandage with him, so maybe he was a doctor on his way to make rounds or to attend a medical convention. Maybe he was just taking a little vacation. Suffice it to say that he likely had a purpose and a destination in mind. People don't just get out on the road for no reason.

Whatever plans this man had, however, were put on hold the moment he came upon someone in need. Keep in mind that helping this man by the side of the road went well beyond a minor diversion. It would entail more than being a few minutes late for whatever appointment the Samaritan was on his way to keep. In fact, he probably had to cancel the appointment, because this project was going to take the entire day. It took time to bandage the man up. Putting the injured man on his donkey meant that the Samaritan would have to walk. More time. The inn was likely out of his way. Once he got the man there, he probably stayed for a while to make sure he would be okay. According to the text, he even came back the next morning, which suggests he stayed overnight nearby, another likely deviation from his original plan. As if that weren't enough, the Samaritan promised to stop by the inn again when he returned to the area, in case the injured man had incurred additional expenses.

Sometimes I wonder how many of us are willing to cancel our plans and appointments when given the opportunity to help a neighbor in need. I also wonder how crucial all our plans and appointments really are. I suspect that some of our schedules and planning calendars are so full because we like the idea of staying busy, not because what we do is actually so important.

I am the first to admit that I need help in this area. It seems that I'm always in a hurry, always in a rush. That's not a good thing. I often make bad decisions when I'm in a hurry, because I don't take the time to think things through and thoroughly assess the situation. Beyond that, if our focus is on what we have to do or where we have to go next, it's likely we will not be looking for—or open to noticing—the opportunities we have to help neighbors who are in need. We're too busy attending meetings or conferences or getting to appointments.

Whenever I preach on this topic or study it, I am reminded of the words "Physician, heal thyself." For when it comes to slowing down and not having every waking minute of every single day spoken for, I need to hear the message as much as anyone. I'll look at my Palm Pilot calendar and see that it's almost totally filled with names and appointments, one after another. Sometimes I'll have more than one thing going on at the same time, and I don't have any idea how that's supposed to work.

A few years ago, I checked my Palm Pilot calendar and saw that I had a meeting scheduled at 7:30 the next morning with someone named Tim Devo. I had no idea who Tim was or where we were supposed to meet or what the meeting was about. I remember hoping that Tim, whoever he was, would come to my office so I wouldn't stand him up someplace else. Fortunately, at 6:30 in the morning, an hour before the meeting, I got a call on my cell phone reminding me that people were expecting me to lead devotions that morning at Timothy Christian High School. "Tim Devo" was short for Timothy Christian devotions. The incident served to remind me that when our calendars include names and appointments we don't even recognize, we are probably overbooked.

Sometimes I think I need a 12-Step program designed specifically for people who are addicted to busyness and hurry. I would walk in and say, "Hello. My name is Wayne, and I pack so much into my planning calendar that I have no time left for anyone, including people who may need my help the most. And I want to change." Unfortunately, my wife, Anne, has carried the brunt of the difficulty of my overbooked schedule. There have been times when I'm doing my journaling or praying, and God speaks to me about this problem. His message on these occasions is clear: I need to understand that it's more important to have time to help a neighbor in need than to have a packed schedule.

We need to start scheduling less so that we will be available to help others when we have the opportunity. This might mean saying no to things we've said yes to before. It might even mean offending some people, but that's the risk we take if we decide to realign our priorities.

Beyond scheduling less, when we have an opportunity to help a neighbor, we, like the Good Samaritan, need to be willing to change our plans and cancel our appointments instead of just walking by on the other side of the road.

I know of someone who tells the story of an important manila folder that he misplaced. This was no ordinary folder. It contained all of his most pressing priorities, "must do" action items, and most needed and timely information. Though he felt lost without it, after searching for over an hour he finally gave up in despair.

Several months later, he was moving some office furniture, and he found the folder, which had fallen behind a filing cabinet. He looked again at what he had thought were high priorities and realized they were not so important after all. Some of them he had remembered to do, and some went undone, but no one was any worse for his having lost track of his high-priority folder. The lesson here is that the things we think are important may not be so important after all.

Our neighbors are people who may need more than just a little bit of our time. Maybe we should include in our planning calendars unscheduled time during which we can pursue opportunities God has placed before us to help our neighbors who are in need. And, like the Good Samaritan, we need to be open to stopping to help another even if it means being late or canceling altogether. What, after all, is most important in God's eyes?

26

My Neighbor Is Visible

The way Jesus' parable of the Good Samaritan is worded makes clear the cause-and-effect relationship between the priest and the Levite *seeing* the beaten man by the side of the road and their moving to the other side so they could avoid him. Had they not made visual contact with the beaten man, this would be a different story. It would be hard to hold the priest and the Levite accountable for their actions (or rather their inaction) had they passed by without noticing the beaten man—had they not even realized he was there.

Our neighbors are people who are visible to us—people we can see as we walk along our daily paths in life. Some of them we might see on a regular basis; others we might come upon only occasionally. With still other neighbors, we might have just one opportunity to stop and help.

To some, it may seem trivial or obvious to point out that we are able to help only those people of whom we are aware, those we can see. But to me as a pastor this is an important point. For there are some pastors who seem to make a living out of making people feel guilty. They dwell on the many problems all around the world in an effort to "guilt" people into doing something or perhaps giving money to some cause.

Every day there are unseen people starving, unseen children being abused, and unseen workers being discriminated against in the workplace that we can't do anything about. I don't believe that those who teach the Word of God ought to be making people feel guilty about those things over which they have little, if any, control. Rather, my aim is to help people understand the truth of God's Word. The centerpiece of this truth is that God loves all people more than any of us can imagine or completely grasp. When we experience this love and accept it, we will be motivated to respond by sharing God's love with others.

If our hearts have been properly prepared, then when we see our neighbors in need, we will respond as God wants us to respond, not as the priest and the Levite responded. I like the way THE MESSAGE translation of the Bible describes what the priest and the Levite did. It states that the priest "angled to the other side" and that the Levite "also avoided the injured man." Somehow, "angled" communicates something beyond merely "going" or "walking" to the other side. It suggests a sort of slyness or an awareness of hypocrisy. The priest and the Levite couldn't just be honest and admit that on that day their actions did not live up to their calling as religious leaders. Instead, they "angled" and "avoided," pretending not to see what they clearly saw. This description suggests both that their actions were intentional and that they wanted to make sure no one noticed their choice to ignore the man who had been beaten.

People respond to what they see. Consider, for example, the Civil Rights movement of the 1960s. For years, discrimination and abuse had been taking place in certain parts of our country, especially the South. But it was not until people began to see in their newspapers and on their TV sets images of peace-minded African-American people being beaten with clubs or hosed off their feet by powerful streams of water that the conscience of the broader American public began to awaken.

Many Christian people today respond to what they see, whether the neighbor in need is right next door or halfway around the world. Christian relief and development organizations have learned that by televising images—especially of children who eke out a living day after day with little hope of a better tomorrow—they can inspire fellow Christians to support efforts to alleviate the suffering.

I will always be proud of my own congregation for its response to Hurricane Katrina victims. One Sunday, we took up an offering to do our part to help. This was not announced ahead of time, so people weren't prepared. Even though we are far from a wealthy congregation, we gave $7,500 that morning. And since this special offering had no negative effect on regular giving to the church, I knew that the over-and-above amount represented significant sacrifices on the part of the people of Lawndale Community Church. On that morning, neighbors in need were visible, and God's people responded out of loving obedience.

While I do not want people to feel guilty about what they don't see, and thus can't do anything about, I do want us to guard against the tendency to hide from the world, to deny that there is suffering and need, and to run away from it. Have you ever noticed, for example, that nursing homes are always located in out-of-the-way areas? These are places where people are old and sick, and many of them suffer from dementia and incredible loneliness. We know these places are there, but we never see them because our society prefers to hide them from clear, accessible view.

I'm reminded of the guy who hears his car making a new and unusual grinding noise, suggesting that something is wrong. Instead of taking the car to a mechanic to have it checked out, the driver simply turns up the volume on his radio and, like magic, the grinding noise disappears. But it's only the noise that goes away, not the problem.

To a great extent, we are able to choose how much of the world we want to see and how much we want to shield from our view. I recognize that there may be a fine line between making people feel guilty and challenging people to keep their eyes open so they can see what God would have them see. But this is not so much a matter of guilt as it is a matter of spiritual maturity.

Many Christians, including me, begin each day with a prayer asking God to be with us, to lead us on that day. "God, here's my day," we pray. "Take it. Make it Your day. Use me. I'll do anything You want me to do with my life today. I'm Yours. Fill me with Your Holy Spirit. I want to serve You this day."

The hymn "Spirit of the Living God" includes the words "melt me, mold me, fill me, use me." Another song petitions, "Open my eyes, Lord, I want to see Jesus." Well, if we truly want to see Jesus, we can see Him in the eyes of the widow, and of the lonely man in the nursing home, and of the hungry child. When we serve a neighbor in need, we are serving Jesus.

The apostle Paul instructs, "Do nothing out of selfish ambition or vain conceit. Rather, in humility value others above yourselves" (Philippians 2:3, *TNIV*). With this in mind, spiritually mature Christians don't hide from problems or try to angle to the other side of the road. They pray for opportunities to serve. They ask God to make visible a neighbor who needs a word of encouragement or a helping hand. I believe that when we ask God for these opportunities, God provides the wisdom and resources we need to respond faithfully. I hope you will consider asking God to make visible to you people—neighbors near or far—who need your love today.

27

My Neighbor Is a Victim

The man who was beaten up and left to die on the side of the road was a victim. He was the target of a crime, and a violent one at that. If we define "victim" as someone who has been wrongly harmed or who has experienced some sort of injustice, then I suspect that every person reading these words has been a victim at some point in their lives.

All of us, I suspect, have been harmed by others, sometimes perhaps even by those in this world who are supposed to love us the most. Children can be victims of abusive or neglectful parents. Virtually every day in U.S. cities, people become victims of crimes ranging from petty theft to rape and murder. And more and more we hear about people who have been victimized by identity thieves or fraudulent investment schemes.

We can be victims of another person's unkind or insensitive words. We can be victims of discrimination in the workplace. Later I will mention a victim of our criminal justice system—someone who was falsely accused and wrongly imprisoned.

It's likely that the main characters in the parable of the Good Samaritan were also victims. Samaritans were victims of the hatred of Jews, who would walk by on the other side of the road in order to avoid talking to or acknowledging a Samaritan. They were shunned, pushed aside, not welcome. Thus the Good Samaritan was himself a victim.

We ought to consider the possibility that the priest and the Levite, too, had at some point in their lives been victims. Perhaps they, like most people then and now, had been harmed or injured in ways that made it challenging for them to show kindness to others—that made it hard for them to do what they should have done.

Some people find it difficult to push through the pain of their "victimhood" in order to help others. They are stuck in their own sense of victimization. We all know people who say, "I can't help anyone else because of what I'm going through." Every time we are with such persons, it seems the constant refrain is, "Woe is me. Look what happened to me." Often such persons adopt a "victim mentality," according to which they take no responsibility for their own mistakes, failures or shortcomings. They just can't bring themselves to say, "I messed up. I made a mistake." Instead, they are always the victim, and it's always somebody else's fault that whatever happened.

In coming to the aid of someone in need, the Good Samaritan rose above any victim mentality he may have had. With this in mind, I believe that, through the parable of the Good Samaritan, Jesus teaches us that we've got to escape whatever sense of victimization we may have long enough to help other victims whom we see. It might even be that helping others is good therapy—that it's the best way to free ourselves from our own victimization, since helping another takes the focus off ourselves and our own problems and issues.

Stanley, the minister of music at Lawndale Community Church, has as much right as anyone I know to claim victimization. Two years after Stanley was unjustly imprisoned, the governor of Illinois granted him clemency because he knew that Stanley should never have gone to prison in the first place.

I've never once witnessed Stanley shirking any responsibility or making excuses or being bitter, even though the justice system did him wrong. He's put it all behind him. In fact, Stanley has challenged people in the church to take note of what Paul says in his second letter to the Corinthians. Paul states that the God of all comfort "comforts us in all our troubles, so that we can comfort those in any trouble with the comfort we ourselves have received from God" (2 Corinthians 1:4). In verse six, he continues, "If we are distressed, it is for your comfort and salvation."

Paul has been going through some pretty tough times, but his focus is not on himself or his own troubles. Instead, he sees a purpose behind his own struggles, namely, that he will be better equipped to comfort others.

We can't change what has happened to us. We can't undo the past. But we *can* see to it that past incidents of victimization do not paralyze us. As long as we remain enslaved by our victimization, we won't be able to obey Jesus and love our neighbors. All we can think about is the bad things that have happened to us.

I want to be careful not to minimize the pain associated with having been a victim, especially if it is the result of some traumatic experience. We have to process those things and work through them, sometimes with the help of a good counselor. That can take time. But at some point, we need to trust in the power of Jesus to help us rise above our circumstances and overcome the effects of whatever harm or injustice we experienced. Healing can be found in reaching out to others in need.

I challenge you today to put your past behind you and to ask Jesus to help you focus not on yourself, but on other victims, especially those for whom the wounds may still be fresh. Whom do you know who is a victim—who has been injured, cheated out of something they deserve, forced to live in substandard housing, or simply bombarded by the common problems of life to a point where they feel they've had all they can bear? Such victims are your neighbors. Extend a hand of love to them and you may just find yourself thinking less and less about your own victimization. More importantly, you will be doing what Jesus calls us to do.

28

My Neighbor Is Someone Who's Been Violated

To say that something bad happened to the man who was eventually helped by the Good Samaritan does not paint an accurate enough picture. After all, bad things happen to most people virtually every day. We shake it off, forget about it, and don't lose any sleep over it, figuring that tomorrow we can get a brand new start.

There is, however, a world of difference between merely experiencing something bad and being violated. Think about someone you know who's been in a car accident. No one is seriously injured, but the car is totaled. What a hassle it is to have to find a new car and perhaps deal with police and insurance companies.

A car accident is a bad thing to experience, but it cannot compare to the experience of being violated. To be violated is to come face to face with human evil. It's to be victimized in a way that is very hard to overcome. It's not something people can merely shake off in the hope that tomorrow will be better. Being violated entails a certain loss of innocence—innocence that is replaced by a kind of fear and insecurity that for some may never go away completely.

It would have been one thing if the man who long ago needed help had simply taken a bad fall or maybe been kicked and stepped on by his mule. He still would have been physically wounded and in need of help. But because he had been violated, his injuries went well beyond the physical. He was without doubt injured spiritually and emotionally as well. Among other things, his ability to trust other people had been dealt a major blow.

When I consider this whole concept of being violated, the evil that immediately comes to mind is the crime of rape. Rape cannot be fairly described simply as a bad thing that happened to someone. It goes far beyond that. Rape entails taking a wonderful gift from God—a gift meant to be shared by men and women in the context of marriage—and turning it into a violent, dehumanizing offense. By no means is this violation something a person can simply shake off. Trust has been broken; innocence has been lost.

It pains me to think about some of the statistics associated with the violation of rape. According to those statistics, in the United States, on average, someone is raped or sexually assaulted every two and a half minutes. That means if you go to church for an hour and half, 36 people will be sexually assaulted during the time you're there. One in every six people is a victim of sexual assault. So if you go to a concert or athletic event where there are 600 people, statistically speaking, 100 of those people either have experienced or will experience sexual assault.

Most of the victims are women, but males can be raped, too. Men in prison are sometimes sexually assaulted by other men. Forty-four percent of sexual assault victims are under the age of 18, while 80 percent are under the age of 30. While sexual assault is a horrible offense regardless of the demographics, it is especially tragic when the victims are young people whose emotions are tender and who are still finding their place in this world.

As a pastor, I have from time to time spoken with and attempted to help people who have been violated by the crime of rape. Typically they have trouble talking about the experience, which makes it difficult for them to put it behind them. Regardless of whether or not it seems logical, people who've been raped tend to feel ashamed, embarrassed, guilty, worthless and broken-hearted. Often they blame themselves. They have trouble imagining their emotions ever returning to some semblance of normality.

I have listened as rape victims tell their stories. It generally doesn't take long for the tears to well up in them. Once they start crying, they can't stop, and inevitably I am moved to tears as well. To deal with the consequences of being violated in this way is a daunting task. People who have been violated by sexual assault are aptly described in Psalm 34: their hearts have been broken, their spirits crushed. It's as if the person who violated them threw a huge boulder on top of them and crushed them into the ground. But Psalm 34 also tells us that God is near to the broken-hearted, and that God comes alongside and helps those who are crushed in spirit. And one of the ways God does this is through members of the Body of Christ—people like you and like me. People who have been violated are our neighbors. God wants us to come alongside them, to walk with them, to accompany them.

We do so not as expert psychologists who have all the answers, nor as magicians who can make their pain and heartache some-how disappear. The truth is that it's okay if we don't know exactly what to do or say. In fact, I've often told my congregation that I love it when somebody says to me, "I don't know how to do it. I feel inadequate." My experience has taught me that this is the kind of person who will be successful in helping others. On the other hand, I get scared when somebody takes an approach that suggests that he or she has all the answers. Assuring a rape victim that she did nothing wrong and that God loves her, then giving her a hug and sending her on her way will not be enough to meet her need. It just doesn't work that way with people who have been violated so severely.

Many churches, including Lawndale Community Church, are part of the Stephen Ministry movement. Lay persons who feel called to support those in the midst of difficult life situations receive training so they know how to help. My wife, Anne, is one of the Stephen Ministry leaders at Lawndale Community Church. She has helped to train members of our congregation to be present with people going through a difficult time, to walk alongside, to listen. One of the things people learn is that there are no quick and easy answers.

Not having answers or solutions, however, is no reason to avoid the person who has been violated. When we see someone who is hurting coming down the road, we can be tempted to pass by on the other side. We don't want to start a conversation because we don't know what to say. We don't have any answers.

Many times, the best "answer" is simply to walk alongside a neighbor who has been violated and to listen if he or she needs someone to talk to. Perhaps you can send the person a card to let her know you're thinking about her, and that you care, and that she is special.

Do you know someone who has been violated? Perhaps it happened recently or maybe months or even years ago? That person is your neighbor, someone who, even when there are no answers to be found, needs someone to walk alongside her tenderly and lovingly.

29

My Neighbor Is Vulnerable

To be vulnerable is to be defenseless. Those among us who are most vulnerable are those who are least able to protect themselves, not just from other people but from the many storms of life.

We don't know how vulnerable the man who was beaten and left on the side of the road was prior to the assault. Perhaps he was very vulnerable—small in stature, perhaps elderly or partially physically disabled. But regardless of how vulnerable he was before he was accosted, we know he was desperately vulnerable afterwards, having been beaten, robbed and stripped. He was vulnerable to everything, from heat exhaustion due to the blazing desert sun, to an animal coming up to take a bite out of him, to another person showing up intent on seeing if he had anything left to steal.

When I think of people today who are the most vulnerable, among those I think of are the youngest and the oldest people: children and the elderly. In some ways, the elderly are more vulnerable. At least with babies and young children, we are generally aware that they need care and attention. It's easier to forget the elderly, especially since these are people who at one time—perhaps not long ago—were perfectly able to take care of themselves.

But even more vulnerable than children and the elderly are children who have yet to be born. In most cases, at least younger people and older people have a voice—some possibility of asking for help. Unborn children have no such voice.

Since the passage of *Roe v. Wade* in the 1970s, our country has averaged approximately one million abortions every year. Around the world, there are about 46 million abortions each year. As I read and study the Scriptures, I can only conclude that life itself is a precious gift; that it's something to be valued, cherished and protected. So I'm saddened by our culture's disregard for life, as evidenced by the loss of a million unborn children each year in the U.S.

Many people think of abortion as a contemporary issue, a modern reality. Actually it's been practiced going back at least to New Testament times. Jesus and the early Church were under the authority of the Roman Empire. And within the Roman Empire, it was legal to abort babies. In fact, the Romans actually went one step further. Those who have studied the history of this era know that there were many more male than female Roman citizens. As is the case in some cultures today, women were not valued as highly as men. So if a baby happened to be a little girl instead of a boy, it was okay by Roman law to kill that baby.

An early Christian document called the *Didache* was written in the context of this reality. The *Didache* is not part of the Bible, but it was considered an important document for the early Church, much as Christian books and Bible commentaries might help us along the way today. Written near the close of the first century by an unknown author, the 16 chapters of the *Didache* addressed several issues of importance to the Church. Most likely, according to scholars, it was written by someone who lived very near Antioch, the place where a racially diverse community of Christ followers deeply committed to loving their neighbors was first called "Christian."

The second chapter of the *Didache* addresses "grave sins." Now, we know, theologically speaking, that sin of any kind—grave or not—separates us from God, and that Jesus' sacrificial death bridges that gap. But the *Didache* defines a "grave sin" as the kind of sin that has long-term effects not just on the person who committed the sin, but on others, too. For example, the grave sin of murder obviously affects the person whose life was wiped out, and the grave sin of adultery affects not just the sinner, but the entire family.

I offer this information about the *Didache* mainly because, in the context of the Roman Empire's culture of death, the *Didache* specifically instructs believers that they should neither murder a child by abortion nor kill a child who has been born. These are considered grave sins. The early Christian community was decidedly pro-life. In caring for their neighbors, Christ followers took a stand in favor of the vulnerable.

As much as anyone, and more than most, Mother Teresa was a neighbor to unborn children. At the National Prayer Breakfast on February 5, 1994, in front of government officials, including the President, and before a nation that had legalized abortion, as a follower of Christ she offered these words:

"It is not enough for us to say, 'I love God,' but I also have to love my neighbor. St. John says that you are a liar if you say you love God and you don't love your neighbor. How can you love God whom you do not see, if you do not love your neighbor whom you see, whom you touch, with whom you live? . . . This requires that I be willing to give until it hurts. Otherwise, there is not true love in me and I bring injustice, not peace, to those around me."

She went on to say, "But I feel that the greatest destroyer of peace today is abortion, because it is a war against the child, a direct killing of the innocent child, murder by the mother herself. And if we accept that a mother can kill even her own child, how can we tell other people not to kill one another? How do we persuade a woman not to have an abortion? As always, we must persuade her with love and we remind ourselves that love means to be willing to give until it hurts. Jesus gave even His life to love us. So, the mother who was thinking of abortion, should be helped to love, that is, to give until it hurts her plans, or her free time, to respect the life of her child. The father of that child, whoever he is, must also give until it hurts."

Last, she said this: "Please don't kill the child. I want the child. Please give me the child. I am willing to accept any child who would be aborted and to give that child to a married couple who will love the child and be loved by the child." .

Those of us who would be neighbors to the vulnerable should be bold to speak up for unborn children who are unable to defend themselves. Our responsibility doesn't end there, however. We ought also to recognize the vulnerability of women who have had abortions. They are frequently vulnerable to the burdens of guilt, sadness and grief. God does not give up on anyone, regardless of what that person has done or failed to do.

One of the most moving speakers we have had at Lawndale is a woman from Denver named Patricia Raybon, author of the book *I Told the Mountain to Move*. In a chapter on confession, she focuses on James 5:16: "Confess your sins to each other and pray for each other so that you can live together whole and healed" (*THE MESSAGE*).

In her introductory paragraph in this chapter, Patricia writes, "So I confess now. I have to. After everything else, I can't go further until I tell the whole and final truth. So I confess it. I confess. With my own mouth, I confess: I aborted two babies. My own baby angels. Sweet little things, so sweet I believe they just melted into heaven, falling like rose petals into the Father's big hands."

This is the most honest treatment from someone who's had an abortion that I've ever read or heard. Patricia openly acknowledges her regret, her guilt, and her grief for the children who were lost to abortion. She writes, "I had told myself that an abortion would end my problems, not complicate them by bringing an innocent life into my own upheaval. I swallowed Satan's lie, that is, then spit it out again, saying it with my own mouth."

She ends the chapter by writing a letter to the babies who were aborted:

Dear Babies:
    This is Mama. You will know my voice, I think, even though we were together for such a short time. I did a bad thing. I didn't trust God.

I didn't understand that God would have made every-thing okay. I was like Peter, [who] . . . looked at the waves, not at Jesus. And when he looked at the waves, he started to sink—down, down, down.

That's how I felt, like I was sinking down.

When the doctors said you were growing inside of me, that's how I felt, so I didn't love myself enough to know how to love you. I was afraid. Oh babies, I had made so many, many mistakes. And I was afraid.

So I let fear convince me that more babies would just make things worse.

Instead, look what I did.

I robbed us. First, I robbed you—taking your own lives. Your own Mama! I didn't think I was strong enough. So I robbed myself of all the joy you would've brought me too. Brought all of us, your sisters, your family, and for each of you, your daddy. I thought we'd have more problems. That we didn't have enough money. That we didn't have enough time. That we didn't have enough love. But I just didn't know then that God is bigger. And God would make everything all right. I didn't know . . .

I know you are in heaven, waiting for us—waiting for me.

I know you've been waiting, looking every day, won-dering when I would get there. Oh, babies, I'm trying to get there—to be better, to live right, to be right, to learn what God wants me to learn, so I can make it to you.

Our neighbors are people who are vulnerable—people who need us to stand up for them when they are unable to stand on their own. Among them are elderly persons and children—born and unborn. But let us not forget those who are trying their best to pick up the pieces from mistakes made in the past. They are our neighbors, too.

30

My Neighbor Is a Human Being

At first glance, stating that the man who was beaten up and left to die on the side of the road was a human being seems so clear and obvious that it is hardly worth mentioning. It's like saying, "The sky is blue." It's a true enough statement, but it's not very helpful since everyone knows the color of the sky.

I am not convinced, however, that people (including Christians) fully comprehend the implications of what it means to be human. Just look around at the ways human beings treat other human beings. I'm not talking just about being impolite, rude or inconsiderate of others' feelings. Beyond this, people rob and murder other people. We tolerate unjust public policies and social attitudes that negatively affect other human beings. Human beings from one nation or political group drop bombs on and shoot guns at human beings from another nation or political group.

In today's world, one should not have to look very far to conclude that something is severely lacking in our theology of humanity. To put it another way, if all people truly and fully understood what it means to be created by God as human beings—and the ramifications for how we should treat others—the violence and injustice and insensitivity that surround us would disappear fairly quickly.

We need to come to a fuller appreciation of what the Bible teaches from the very beginning. These days, the short phrase, "It's all good!" seems to be in vogue. That statement originated with God, in Genesis, chapter one. Each day, after creating something new, God ended the day by pronouncing, simply, "And it was good."

What a beautiful, wondrous world God created—the sun, moon and stars; the birds of the air and the fish of the sea; the flowers and trees; and all the animals. But the crowning achievement of God's creation was human beings. We read in Genesis 1:27, "Let us create human beings in our image." And at the end of the sixth day, after creating human beings, God didn't just say, "It was good." He said, "It was very good."

Men and women are thus unique in all of creation. Human beings—and human beings alone—bear the image of God. This makes us far more important than the most brilliant star, the most majestic mountain, or the most colorful bird. How differently human beings would treat one another if we fully understood that human beings uniquely bear the image of God.

This understanding might also make a difference in the kinds of causes we get involved in and the passion with which we pursue them. Christian people get behind myriad causes as part of an effort to help make this world a better place. Not all of these causes have to do with church work, nor are they all sponsored by churches or Christian organizations. But Christians who are involved in any cause, whether or not a Christian organization is behind it, are motivated by their faith and their efforts to do God's will. It makes perfect sense, for example, for a Christ follower to advocate recycling programs and other efforts to care for our environment. After all, in Genesis 1:28, God tells us that we are the stewards of our world. We are to rule over the fish of the sea, the birds of the air, and the animals that walk on land. As Christians, we are trusted to care for the earth. For a believer to be an environmentalist ought to be a foregone conclusion.

As we get involved in various causes, however, we would do well to remember that the most important and urgent causes are those rooted in understanding that our neighbors are human beings who were created in the image of God and who continue to bear the image of God. Thus we must resist any urge to be program-oriented if it limits our capacity to be people-oriented. Keeping in mind the words of Isaiah 11:4—"But with righteousness he will judge the needy, with justice he will give decisions for the poor of the earth"—in everything we do, we have a responsibility to consider how what we do will affect other people.

We are called to live righteous lives. This righteousness includes particular concern and care for those who have been treated unjustly or unlovingly. We are to strive to make justice available to everyone, and we're called to care for those who are less fortunate than ourselves, namely, those who are poor, including the poor in spirit.

Since writing *The Purpose-Driven Life*, which is second in sales only to the Bible, Rick Warren, pastor of Saddleback Church in Lake Forest, California, has said that God awakened his heart to the struggles of hurting people in our world. During the 2008 election season, Warren convened a group of leaders to talk about the subject of HIV/AIDS. His goal was to bring to the table anyone who wanted to make a difference in this particular effort to alleviate human suffering. He invited people who would normally not be on the same side of political or social issues. He invited then-presidential candidate Barack Obama, but also conservative Republican Kansas Senator Sam Brownback.

I was one of a couple hundred pastors from around the country invited to spend the day with Pastor Warren prior to his AIDS conference. He shared that he had received a lot of criticism from the right and the left. His response was that he did not favor either the right or the left wing. Rather, his concern was for the whole bird. In taking the approach he took, I believe Warren understood that we as the Church are called to bring people together—even though they might disagree on various issues—wherever we see an opportunity to address human suffering and injustice. Sometimes we allow the world to define our agenda, to divide based on politics, and to keep us from recognizing that Christians should be united behind any cause rooted in a sound theology of humanity.

Warren has come up with what he calls the "five global Goliaths" that he believes the human race, particularly followers of Jesus, ought to combat. I hope that all those who understand the implications of the humanity of the man who was beaten up and left on the side of the road will make these "global Goliaths" priorities as we choose our causes.

The first global Goliath is spiritual emptiness. People don't know God. The second is egocentric leadership. Many people, when they get power, become corrupt. It's a worldwide problem. The third Goliath is extreme poverty. Every night, all over the world, people go to bed hungry. Those who believe that all human beings bear the image of God should find this unacceptable. We are called to come alongside those who are threatened by hunger and starvation.

The fourth is pandemic disease, including AIDS. When we first heard about AIDS in the 1980s, it seemed that if someone tested positive for the HIV virus, that person died fairly quickly. Thank God that, while there is still no cure, modern medicine has developed drugs that enable people with AIDS to live normally for a long time. When basketball great Magic Johnson was diagnosed with AIDS in the mid '90s, most people thought he would die within a year or so, and he probably thought he would too. But thanks to modern medicine, he is still doing well and living his life. However, people around the world die every day of curable or at least treatable diseases because they do not have access to the medical care and the drugs they need to survive.

Warren's fifth Goliath is illiteracy and poor education. Both here in the U.S. and around the globe, people who cannot read or do not have some basic education are increasingly finding it hard to survive, let alone thrive, in a global economy. Helping neighbors who bear the image of God learn to fend for themselves ought to be near the top of our list of causes, as so often poverty and education level go hand in hand.

Poverty is no longer a city thing. In the Chicago area, there are now more poor people living in the suburbs than in the city. This is due in part to the fact that as housing projects are torn down, people relocate to the suburbs. "Urban ministry" is no longer synonymous with ministry to the poor. We need to work to bridge what has been called the "digital divide." By this I mean that in affluent areas, virtually every home with a child in school has access to a computer. In poverty-stricken areas, only about one in ten homes enjoys such access. This digital divide, which is a reality in cities, suburbs and rural areas, serves to further isolate and marginalize the poor.

I encourage all followers of Christ to become involved in as many causes as they are able. In choosing those causes, always remember that it's about people. Whatever and whenever we tear down or build up, we should consider the ramifications for people. We need to be about feeding the hungry, clothing the naked, and working to ensure that all people receive the justice they need and deserve. It all begins with the question, "Who is my neighbor?" and the answer, "My neighbor is a human being who bears the image of God."

31

My Neighbor Feels Humiliated

I want you to exercise your powers of imagination for a few moments. Go deep into your feelings and emotions. Do your best to put yourself in the place of the man who was beaten and left to die on the side of the road. Imagine you've been shopping all day, and time has gotten away from you. You have a long walk to your car, and given the time of day, it's not as safe a walk as you'd like it to be. You're halfway there when someone jumps out in front of you and clubs you with a baseball bat, knocking you down.

You're a bit woozy and bleeding. This violent robber proceeds to smack you around a few times, kicking you in the face and stomach. You're in pain and you feel very scared, too scared to be angry. Then he begins to take all your possessions—your cash, credit cards, driver's license, watch, jewelry, even your eyeglasses. You feel helpless, but not yet humiliated.

Then he begins to tear your clothes off, and he takes them all until you are totally naked, with nothing to cover up with. Now, even if the assailant leaves the scene without harming you further, you are in very bad shape. You hope someone comes along soon to help you, but if and when that happens, you will feel completely embarrassed and humiliated. This is because the person who attacked you didn't only take all your possessions; he also stole your self-esteem.

To be humiliated is to have our self-esteem stripped away. Our neighbors are those to whom this very thing has happened. They are people who have been stripped of their dignity—who feel embarrassed and humiliated, so much so that it's hard to face others.

I count it a privilege to have among my friends a number of people who have gone to prison. I like to be able to know people from all walks of life—rich and poor, people from different countries, and people who come from different backgrounds. I know people who were born into privilege and others who have had to struggle since the day they were born. And yes, some of my friends have done prison time. Some of them were falsely accused and convicted. Others recognize that they did something wrong and are determined to learn from their mistakes and move forward. To be labeled an "ex-con" carries with it a certain stigma. At least a bit of humiliation comes with the territory.

It's not just the prisoners, but also their families who experience humiliation. One of my ex-convict friends is not from Lawndale and does not fit the stereotypical image of someone who has gone to prison. I knew him before, during and after his prison experience and called him my friend the entire time. While he was imprisoned, he did okay. The experience was not as bad for him as one might think the prison experience would be. In many ways, he grew while in prison; he became a better person. It was in prison that he first began to spend some serious time reading the Bible. He also learned to pray while in prison. In fact, he spent a couple of hours each day in prayer. All in all, being in prison, while somewhat embarrassing and not something he would have wished for himself, was not all that bad, largely because God used this time in this man's life to draw him closer.

The experience, however, was not so easy on my friend's wife, who felt completely humiliated by having a husband who was in jail. Whether she was walking to church, to the corner store, or around the block for some exercise, she could not shake the feeling—legitimate or imagined—that people were whispering about her and her situation.

Things were even tougher on the children. Junior high and high school can be brutal years for kids under normal circumstances, but imagine what it is like for children whose father is in jail. What do they say when people ask, "How come we never see your dad? What does he do?" The hurt and humiliation for this family were intense and real.

In an earlier chapter, I referred to the privilege we have each year at Lawndale of participating in the Angel Tree program, which gives our church the chance to visit with between 1,000 and 1,500 children whose parents are incarcerated. When the kids come to get their gifts, we do all we can to affirm them so that at least some of the dignity that may have been stripped away can be restored. We try to let them know that, despite any humiliation they have experienced, they are special. The fact that they have a parent in prison is never mentioned; the word "prison" is never even stated. We simply have a great celebration. We make sure that these children receive gifts from their parents, so they know that, even though their mom or dad is away from home, they didn't forget their children. We try to send the message, "Your mom and dad love you because you are special."

Humiliation, of course, can come from many sources. People who suffer from HIV/AIDS, in addition to the physical challenges they face, are commonly ostracized. And, as was the case with Mary more than 2,000 years ago, unmarried women who become pregnant face varying degrees of humiliation depending in part on the circumstances. So do those who experience divorce. Getting fired from a job—or even just getting laid off—can be humiliating. In addition to the practical concerns, those who lose their jobs typically feel a loss of dignity and self-worth.

The man who was beaten and left to die on the side of the road needed someone to come to his rescue. He needed someone to protect him from further danger. He needed someone to take him to a place of safety so that his physical wounds could begin to heal. He also needed someone to walk beside him in the midst of the humiliation he must have felt. Our neighbors are people who for one reason or another have been humiliated. Ministry to such persons requires a special sensitivity—the kind that addresses the need without openly acknowledging it, so as not to open up the wound any further. These neighbors need us to walk beside them in the midst of their humiliation so that their dignity and self-esteem can be restored, and they can find their way back to wholeness.

32

My Neighbor
Feels Hopeless

I heard it said once that the average person can live 40 or so days without food, three days without water, three or four minutes without air, but not a single second without hope. Whether or not you agree, the point is well taken. It's hard for a person to live if that person has lost all hope that whatever pain or situation he or she is in can change.

Our neighbors are people who have lost hope. The man who was beaten and left on the side of the road didn't start off being hopeless. He probably had plenty of hope when he saw the priest approaching. But the priest didn't stop. Same thing with the Levite. The people whose mission in life supposedly was to help others chose not to stop and help. The beaten man probably thought his life was over. He lost hope.

I'm often asked what is the greatest problem facing the Lawndale community. People expect me to respond with something such as "gangs" or "crime" or "gentrification" or "drugs." I usually surprise them when I tell them what I think the biggest problem is: "The lack of hope."

Things were not always this way in Lawndale. The community was dealt a major blow in 1968. Emotions erupted and riots broke out following the assassination of Dr. Martin Luther King Jr. The late Chicago-based syndicated newspaper columnist Mike Royko wrote a column about what happened in North Lawndale in April of 1968. He quoted Mayor Daley as making, in the midst of the rioting, the following statement: "I have conferred with the superintendent of police [about this] and I gave him the following instructions: I said to him very emphatically and very definitely that an order be issued by him immediately and under his signature to shoot to kill any arsonist or anyone with a Molotov cocktail in his hand because they are potential murderers, and to issue a police order to shoot to maim or cripple anyone looting any stores in our city."

Stores began to close. Within a few years, the job-providing factories run by Western Electric and International Harvester were gone. Sears moved its headquarters downtown. Thriving businesses were replaced by boarded-up buildings, and there were empty spaces where structures once stood, prior to being torched by arsonists. Residents left in droves. The place where Dr. King stayed when he was in Chicago became a vacant lot.

Author Nicholas Lehman offers some insights into Lawndale's hopelessness in his book *The Promised Land*, which chronicles the migration of African Americans from the South, particularly Mississippi, to Chicago, including the North Lawndale neighborhood. We know that many people came to North Lawndale from Clarksdale, Mississippi. Among those who came from Clarksdale was the Henry family, who, as did many others, remained in Lawndale even after things turned bad because they didn't have the money to move. After interviewing Mrs. Henry in his book, Lehman concluded with the statement, "Any shred of hope that Lawndale had of being a decent neighborhood was now gone."

If people are hungry, we can give them food. If they don't know how to read but are willing to learn, we can teach them. But ministry to those who have lost hope is far more complicated. In thinking about hope and hopelessness, I've been fascinated by something known as the "Stockdale Paradox," a term coined by Jim Collins in his contemporary classic book *Good to Great*.

The Stockdale paradox, as described in Collins's book, derives its name from former Vietnam POW Jim Stockdale, the highest-ranking military officer to be captured by the North Vietnamese. Stockdale was tortured 20 times during his eight years (1965-73) in captivity. In his book, Collins discusses his interview with Stockdale, during which he posed the question, "Who didn't make it out [of the POW camp]?"

Stockdale answered, "Oh, that's easy. The optimists."

Collins was perplexed. So was I upon reading this for the first time. I thought, as most people do, that the thing you would need most in a prison camp would be optimism, since optimists never give up hope. But Stockdale had a different take on this. After Collins expressed his confusion, Stockdale explained that the optimists, at the beginning of their time in the prison camp, were convinced they would be out by Christmas. But Christmas came and went, and they were still POWs. Then they thought they would be out by Easter. Easter came and went, and they were still in captivity. Next they looked toward Thanksgiving. Still no change in their status. Maybe it would be the next Christmas. It was the optimists, who were unable to accept and deal with the reality of their circumstances, who were the first to give up.

The lesson of the Stockdale paradox is that we should not confuse confident faith that will prevail in the end with mere flippant optimism. Sometimes life requires that we see reality as it is and not through those proverbial rose-colored glasses. Collins advises that in every situation we must be careful not to allow optimism to blind us to the brutal facts of our reality, whatever they might be. (According to some researchers, pessimists are more likely than optimists to work to change things for the better, since optimists are more likely to be content with conditions the way they are. This makes sense, given that if you don't admit there's a problem, there's no reason to try to solve it.)

In applying the Stockdale paradox to ministry, as Christians we must be careful not to offer advice that might just make things worse for those we are trying to help. When we see people who are hungry or hurting, feeling humiliated or beaten up by life, we can't just blithely say, "It's all gonna be alright. Everything's gonna work out because God loves you." To do so is to offer false hope.

I have seen this happen as various officials address the problems in our public schools. People express great optimism. They come in and say we're going to do this thing or that thing in order to make the schools better. But then nothing really changes. Unfounded optimism is worthless in the short run and damaging in the long run. When people who are struggling and hurting are disappointed time and again by false hopes that never become reality, they tend to become jaded, weary, and unable to take hold of genuine hope if and when it finally arrives.

Rather than offer false hope and baseless optimism, we need to be honest enough to acknowledge when a situation is hard to cope with or when conditions are difficult. We need to paint a realistic picture. We should follow the lead of the prophet Jeremiah who, in the book of Lamentations, talks candidly about how hard life has been for the children of Israel. To lament (as in Lamentations) is essentially to cry. Jeremiah states, "I remember my affliction . . . I well remember them, and my soul is downcast within me" (Lamentations 3:19-20).

Yes, we must always acknowledge God's immeasurable love and concern for His people. Jeremiah did: "Yet this I call to mind and therefore I have hope. Because of the Lord's great love we are not consumed, for his compassions never fail. They are new every morning; great is your faithfulness" (Lamentations 3:21-23). God's mercies are new every morning. Therein lies the basis for hope. But we should not act as though this will somehow magically relieve people of their pain or frustration. Even as we encourage people to trust in God's love and provision, it's okay to admit when something is hard. In fact, it's more than just okay; it's incumbent on us to do so. Strange as it may seem, the people to whom we are ministering will find some measure of comfort in our honesty. We might not be able to offer much for them to hold on to, but at least what we offer will be real and not just another illusion—one more setup for eventual disappointment.

Another reality that makes ministry to hopeless persons challenging is a phenomenon that has been labeled "conditioned hopelessness," wherein people become, in essence, inoculated against the very possibility of any hope of relief from their difficult circumstances.

Several years ago, psychiatrist Martin Seligman explored this phenomenon through a series of studies with dogs. He took a group of dogs and chained them down in a metal cage so they couldn't move. Then he introduced electricity into the cage, causing the dogs to shake and bark and yelp. They tried to escape, but they couldn't move because they were chained down.

Dr. Seligman continued to introduce electricity. For a while, the dogs had the same reaction, but eventually they became so conditioned that they didn't bark or yelp or try to move. They knew it wouldn't make a difference. Seligman's next step was to take off the shackles before introducing electricity into the cage once again. When he did so, the dogs still didn't bark or yelp or try to move. Even after he swung open the doors to the cage, the dogs reacted the same way: they didn't move. Even after he got other dogs to run about outside the cage to "remind" the subject dogs of what they once could do, the dogs—even with the cage door open—would not move. The dogs were, in essence, victims of conditioned hopelessness.

People, too, can become victims of conditioned hopelessness, which produces the feeling of being trapped—unable to escape the reality of our circumstances. When people continually "pass us by," we are conditioned to be hopeless. This phenomenon might help explain why people harm others who are just like them or why they get hooked on drugs. They've lost hope. And even when some measure of hope is within reach, they don't recognize it because they've been conditioned to not even try to change anything.

However, Dr. Seligman did one more thing. He took an "unconditioned" dog and put it in the cage with the other dogs, which were still unshackled. The cage door was swung open. After Seligman introduced the electricity, the conditioned dogs still did not bark or yelp or move. But the unconditioned dog responded just like the conditioned dogs had done at first. He began to bark and yelp. Seeing the cage door open, he immediately took his leave. Then something amazing happened. One of the conditioned dogs barked, and another one turned his head. Another started to move toward the door. They began to remember what it had been like before they were conditioned to lose hope. Within 30 seconds or so, all of the dogs had moved beyond their conditioned hopelessness and left the cage.

This reminds us of what Jesus did for all of us. We human beings were trapped in sin and in cages of conditioned hopelessness. Jesus left heaven, came to earth and lived among us, and showed us the way out of the hopelessness that had us paralyzed. If we are to be followers of Christ, we are called to enter the cages of others who are victims of conditioned hopelessness. We are called to love them, sensitively and patiently, and to model hope for them until they, too, can walk out of the cages that have kept them silent and immobile. Who is my neighbor? It is the person who has lost hope.

3 3

My Neighbor Is Poor

We don't know how well off the man who was beaten and left on the side of the road was before he was assaulted. But we know that afterwards he had nothing. And there were no insurance policies back then to cover his losses. Everything, including all his money, had been taken from him. He was poor.

I think a lot, as I hope you do, about what it means to be poor in the world today. The devastating earthquake in Haiti in January of 2010 gave the entire world an opportunity to contemplate what it means to be poor. Most people in Haiti, of course, were poor prior to the earthquake. In fact, it was because they were poor that the earthquake took such a heavy toll, especially in human lives. So many people simply could not afford to construct their homes and other buildings in ways that would keep them safe from earthquakes and other natural disasters.

Those of us who live comfortably in the U.S. may find it hard to imagine what it is like to live in poverty. Nor is it easy for us to conceive of how many millions of people around the world wake up each morning wondering what (and sometimes if) they and their families will eat that day. It's been estimated that on any given day 1.3 billion people groan for the possibility of having a cup of clean water.

Such conditions are known as abject poverty, and this kind of poverty affects more than a billion of the world's people, most of them women and children. Sadly, we live in a world where, for the most part, the strong take care of themselves before (sometimes instead of) caring for the weak. Let's not forget that even here in the U.S., and in other developed nations, millions live in poverty. They face difficult choices, for example, between paying for groceries and paying the electric bill. They live in substandard housing if they are not homeless, and they have limited access to even basic medical care.

The music superstar Bono, in his efforts to combat poverty, has noted (as have many others) that caring for the poor constitutes one of Scripture's primary themes. In fact, more than 400 Bible passages, approaching a total of some 4,000 verses, focus in some way on those who are poor, who are disenfranchised or who have been treated unjustly.

With all the attention the Bible pays to the poor, it ought to be clear that God does not want people to be living in poverty or in substandard conditions, and that God does want those who love Him to demonstrate their love by caring for the poor. These related truths are reflected in the Lord's plan for the children of Israel as found in Deuteronomy 15:4, which states, "There should be no poor among you."

I'm aware of Jesus' statement, found in John 12:8, that the poor will always be with us. Unfortunately, some people use this verse to justify a sort of apathy or inaction when it comes to caring for the poor. This is a perfect example of Scripture being taken out of context and misapplied. It's important to understand the difference between descriptive statements (what is) and prescriptive statements (what ought to be). I won't go into all the details, but suffice it to say that in this statement in John, Jesus is in no way saying it's okay to forget about poor people since they'll always be around. This interpretation flies in the face of a major theme of Scripture, namely, that we should care for the poor.

So much of what we do at Lawndale is motivated by our church's concern for the poor. We started our health center because there were people in our neighborhood who did not have access to medical care. We started our development corporation because there were people in our community without access to adequate education, decent housing, and economic opportunity. We have tried to do our part in fulfilling God's desire that, impossible as it may seem to us, no one in the world would be poor.

I am far from alone in thinking that we have enough resources on this planet to accomplish this goal. The problem is that we who are in a position to help are not doing all we can do to achieve the goal. The Lord's message to the people of Israel in Deuteronomy 15:5 is that there would be no poor among them "if only you fully obey the Lord your God and are careful to follow all these commands I am giving you today."

That word "fully" is a very important word. It's easy for us to follow God's commands selectively. It's hard to obey fully. We're more comfortable if we can pick and choose what we want to do and what we want to believe. I tried to make this point several years ago in a speech to seniors at a Christian high school. I asked them to share with me their favorite Bible verses. The Bible teacher there got into the act by revealing that his favorite verse in Scripture was John 10:10. In this verse, Jesus says that the devil comes to steal, kill and destroy, but He came so that people might have life and have it abundantly.

As soon as this Bible teacher revealed his favorite verse, I began to ridicule his choice. I stared him down and said I couldn't believe that someone who claimed to be a Bible teacher could select such a terrible verse as his favorite. I opened my Bible and ripped out the page containing John 10:10, wadded it up, and threw it at him. Believe me, I had every student's attention in that moment! They thought I'd gone crazy.

But then I explained that I also liked John 10:10. I was merely trying to make a point about how many of us treat Scripture. I was illustrating what we do with the verses in the Bible that we don't want to obey—that we prefer to ignore. We simply tear them out of the Bible by not obeying them. That's exactly what the Church as a whole has done by not coming to grips with the Bible's repeated admonitions to care for the poor. It's one of the reasons many people, including Bono, have become disillusioned with the Church.

In a fairly brief span of time I went from not knowing who this Irish rock star Bono was to considering him one of my heroes. I was moved by his song "Pride (In the Name of Love)," written about another of my heroes, Martin Luther King, Jr. The song speaks of shots ringing out in Memphis and about how they could take Dr. King's life, but not his pride. Add to that all Bono has done to help the world's poor—I've even heard him ask the question, "Who is my neighbor?"—and you can understand why I like him so much. Any criticism he offers of the Church doesn't bother me, because it is accurate. In fact, we have an awful lot to learn from people such as Bono.

The Bible states or suggests in various places that, in God's economy, when we serve others, we enrich our own lives. It is common for people to return from a short-term mission trip or a Habitat for Humanity work project saying they received more from those they were helping than they gave. One of the Proverbs states, "Those who give to the poor will lack nothing" (Proverbs 28:27, *TNIV*).

I am convinced that the key to doing well in life is to help somebody who is less fortunate. People wonder why they can never seem to get ahead, and why life is such a struggle. I think often it's because they are not reaching out to those who are less fortunate.

I'm not saying that if a person does something to help a poor family, his or her bank account balance will suddenly skyrocket. I am saying that people who serve the less fortunate with the right motives and a pure heart will find themselves experiencing a kind of joy and contentment that no amount of money or material things can provide.

Proverbs 29:7 states, "The righteous care about justice for the poor, but the wicked have no such concern." It's never a good idea to take a single verse from Scripture and develop an argument based on it. But in this case, the message is consistent with many other Scripture passages. If we want to live righteous lives as followers of

Jesus, we need to care for those who are poor. We are not saved because we care for the poor, but ministry to the poor is an indicator of righteous living that is pleasing to the Lord.

Proverbs 31:8 challenges us especially to "Speak up for those who cannot speak for themselves." This brings to mind those cultures around the world and even some segments of our own American culture where women are treated as second- or third-class citizens. And children anywhere lack the ability to speak for themselves. They depend completely on righteous people to be their voice when they are being abused or at risk of becoming victims of human trafficking.

Proverbs 31 is the chapter that describes the virtuous woman. While we generally regard this proverb as painting a picture of the perfect wife and mother, and the ideal homemaker, let's not forget verse 20, which states, "She opens her arms to the poor and extends her hands to the needy."

Think about Jesus, who, after being baptized and spending forty days in the wilderness, returned to His home synagogue. They handed Him the scroll of Isaiah and told him to read something. He could have picked anything from any of this scroll's 66 chapters. He chose chapter 61, which begins, "The Spirit of the Sovereign Lord is on me, because the Lord has anointed me to proclaim good news to the poor. He has sent me to bind up the brokenhearted, to proclaim freedom for the captives and release from darkness for the prisoners" (Isaiah 61:1, *TNIV*).

I consider this to be our Lord's mission statement. I believe everyone ought to have a mission statement—something that states succinctly why we are here on earth and what we are striving to accomplish. Businesses and nonprofit organizations have mission statements; families and individuals should, too. (My family wrote a mission statement in 1995 that focuses on why the Gordon family exists.)

Lawndale Community Church has a mission statement. We realize we are not like other churches. In most churches, the pastor doesn't wear blue jeans and a Chicago Bears sweatshirt during the sermon. Most churches pass offering plates instead of having a box in the back for those who want to give. We're different because our mission is to reach people who have been turned off to church. You might say we are trying to reach the unchurched of our neighborhood. We don't consider our church to be any better or more righteous than any other church. But we have focused on a distinctive mission.

Another important part of our mission at Lawndale is to serve the poor. This, I believe, ought to be a part of every church's mission statement. After all, we all want to serve Jesus, and He told His followers that when we feed the hungry, reach out to strangers, clothe the naked, care for the sick, and visit the prisoner, we are in fact serving Him (see Matthew 25:35-40). For those Christians who for some reason don't like helping hurting people, including those who are poor, I believe it's time for a faith check.

It's time to follow the example set by people such as Dr. King. It's a mistake to conclude that Dr. King's life and ministry were simply about making things better for black people. His words and his actions demonstrated his concern not just for the members of his own race, but for all people trapped in poverty.

I'm not ashamed to support the efforts of people who are trying to serve the poor, even if they are not known for being people of faith. I've worn a wristband for Bono's One campaign, which has the goal of making poverty history. I applaud the celebrities who came together to raise millions of dollars to help Haiti in its time of greatest need. I thank God that Oprah spent $40 million to build a school for needy children in South Africa, and I'm flabbergasted that anyone would criticize her for doing so. Everyone should be happy that thousands of young people in South Africa will now have opportunities they would not otherwise have had.

It's time for those of us who are believers to examine our own lives and priorities instead of critiquing the behavior or judging the motives of others. Our neighbors are those who are poor. And so I challenge followers of Christ to think about what we are doing to help those who are less fortunate. No matter who you are, where you live, or what you do, you should not have to look far to find many such persons. Chicago is "home" to tens of thousands of homeless persons, and it is by no means unique in this regard. As you bring a smile to the faces of others, you will experience the joy and the surpassing peace that come from serving Christ by serving "the least of these."

34

My Neighbor Is Someone I'm Afraid to Help

No one can say for sure why the priest and the Levite passed right by without giving a second thought to the man who'd been beaten and left on the side of the road. We don't know what they may have been thinking. Most commentators contend that the priest and the Levite were simply too afraid to stop and help. They were afraid that if they hung around there too long, they, too, might get robbed and assaulted.

Our neighbors are those people whom others are afraid to help. They are people who are in some way perceived to be a threat to those who might come to their aid. In Jesus' time, no one would go near a leper. Even if they felt compassion for the lepers, they were too afraid to help. In our day, many people are afraid to get too close to those who have AIDS.

Sometimes we're afraid to put ourselves in situations where we are unsure what to say or do. Thus we have a tendency to avoid people who are confined to wheelchairs or who walk with a limp or who speak in a way that is difficult for us to understand. We know we ought to visit the sick, but it's hard, especially if it's someone in a hospital who's hooked up to all kinds of tubes and machines. We're afraid partly because we don't like to be in situations where we're not in control. We prefer to avoid problems we know we can't solve.

Sometimes we're afraid of other people because of the way they look. Someone might look mean or scary. Or just different. This can be a very subjective thing. A young person with 12 tattoos and 10 piercings might look quite normal to his or her buddies, but frightening to someone from an older generation.

Some people are comforted by the sight of law enforcement officers, while others are fearful because of past experiences of mistreatment. In urban contexts, people are afraid, as they ought to be, of drug dealers and gang leaders. It's important to remember, though, that these people who frighten us are our neighbors and may need our help. So are those persons with mental disabilities or illnesses. It's not uncommon to find such persons walking the streets of our cities. Not long ago, I saw a man standing on the street just talking and talking and talking. At first I thought he had a cell phone, but he didn't. He wasn't talking to me, and there was no one else around. It was a scary thing, because someone who is mentally unstable can be unpredictable. But this man and others like him are our neighbors. Sometimes we just have to try to help and trust Jesus to heal and restore.

You may recall something that happened in January of 2007 that captured the nation's attention. Wesley Autrey, a Navy veteran and construction worker, was waiting for a train at a New York City subway station. He had his two young daughters with him. A 19-year-old student from a film school in the city suffered a seizure and fell down onto the tracks. Wesley saw the light of an oncoming train. He quickly asked a woman standing nearby to keep his daughters at a safe distance. Then he dove onto the tracks.

Wesley was hoping to get the young man off the tracks, but realized he didn't have enough time. So he put the young man in the drainage trench between the tracks, then lay on top of him so he couldn't move. Though the train operator applied the brakes, all but two cars ran over the two men. The bottom of the train got close enough to leave grease on Wesley's cap, but not close enough to do any harm.

Wesley said later that he'd rather try to help someone in danger than allow his daughters to witness someone being killed. He told *The New York Times*, "I don't feel like I did something spectacular; I just saw someone who needed help. I did what I felt was right."

No one would doubt that when Wesley Autrey did what he did, he was afraid. But in spite of his fear, he came to the aid of someone in need. I certainly would not hold it against anyone who would not do what Wesley did in that situation. But I think Wesley's example is something to which we all can aspire.

I challenge you to pay more attention to the situations that scare you and the people of whom you are afraid. Perhaps you fear for your physical safety. Or maybe you're afraid of being embarrassed or taken advantage of. Perhaps your fears are well founded, perhaps not. Either way, these people are your neighbors.

Remember that the antidote to fear is faith. Paul instructs us that "God has not given us a spirit of fear and timidity, but of power, love, and self-discipline" (2 Timothy 1:7, *NLT*), and in Philippians 4:13 he assures us that we can do all things through Christ who strengthens us. I believe that as we grow in our faith, we become less fearful and more bold—more able to face and overcome our fears. Look around you. Who are those people you are too afraid to help? Whom do you shy away from because you are afraid? Remember that they are God's children and your neighbors.

My Neighbor Is Someone Who Is Dangerous to Help

We don't know if the entire road from Jerusalem to Jericho was dangerous, but we can safely assume that some sections, including the spot where the man was beaten and left to die, were unsafe. Perhaps the robber had a good place to hide—behind a tree or a rock. If it was dangerous for the man who was beaten, it might very well have been dangerous for anyone who stopped to help. As noted earlier, this may explain, at least in part, why the priest and the Levite chose to walk away instead of stopping to help. Safety first.

Loving our neighbors will cause us, on occasion, to go to dangerous places. Sometimes I think that, in our American lifestyle and Western culture, we've become obsessed with safety, almost to a point where risk-taking has become a lost art.

Don't get me wrong. I'm all for doing everything we can—taking all precautions—to keep ourselves and others safe. In fact, taking foolish, purposeless risks shows a disrespect for life. We ought to wear seatbelts, for example, to increase the chances that if we are in a car accident, we won't get hurt seriously or at all. Similarly, we have smoke detectors to alert us and help us escape in the event of a fire. As of January 1, 2007, the state of Illinois requires by law that people with furnaces that burn fossil fuels (natural gas) have carbon monoxide detectors. Nothing is to be gained (except saving a few bucks) from ignoring these safety precautions. All of them make perfect sense.

But there is a difference between taking needless risks and choosing to go into harm's way for some worthy cause or noble purpose. Young men and women who have gone to places such as Iraq and Afghanistan over the last several years don't do it because they enjoy taking risks. They are there for a purpose. In taking an aggressive stand on behalf of the poor and disenfranchised, Martin Luther King, Jr. was well aware that he was in danger virtually every day of his life. But he deemed it a risk worth taking.

In contrast, many folks today are so obsessed with staying in a safe environment—so worried about being harmed—that they won't take even the slightest risk, regardless of the reason. If there is the potential for danger, nobody wants to get involved.

I challenge you to think about some of the dangerous places God might be calling you to enter. In Chicago and in other big cities—and even in smaller cities and towns—there are neighborhoods that are considered dangerous. People warn us, "Don't go there." Of course, there are also foreign countries that are considered dangerous. I have actually gone into a few countries in which, upon entering, I saw a big sign stating that the U.S. State Department recommended that no American citizen set foot on this soil. That's quite a warning. But I was there for a reason, and sensed I was supposed to go, so I went.

The fact is that some of the people who live in those dangerous places—whether neighborhoods or countries—are our friends. And many who live or work in these dangerous places are neighbors whom God is calling us to help.

Thousands of U.S. soldiers and tens of thousands of Iraqi citizens have been killed by bombs over the last several years. Iraq is a dangerous place, and it has been for quite some time. Before all the bombing began, a friend of mine from Philadelphia—Shane Claiborne—was praying, and he sensed that God was calling him to go to Iraq. So he did. He actually moved into Baghdad so he could be there with the children of Baghdad and also with Christians who were living there.

Before the bombing started, the U.S. government tried to get every American citizen out of the country. Shane ignored the warning. When the bombing began, he spent most of his time with children. He also found a prayer meeting—a place where he could worship and pray with other Christians. Shane understood that these Iraqi people were human beings created in the image of God, and that they were his neighbors. Without intending for his actions to represent any position on the war, he was willing to take the risk to be with these neighbors in a difficult time.

About a month after Shane returned from Iraq, he came to visit us here at Lawndale. He brought with him a little piece of shrapnel—a piece of metal that had flown off a bomb. When I touched this piece of shrapnel, I was moved to tears. Part of my response was based on fear for innocent people—neighbors—half a world away, who live surrounded by bombs. Most of it was based on realizing that my brother in Christ had risked his own life and wellbeing in response to a compelling call from God.

Most of us are not very far from dangerous places. Perhaps it's that neighborhood where most of the people are from a different ethnic group. Or a street corner where drugs are bought and sold on a regular basis. Those corners that everyone says are dangerous may be some of the very corners God is calling some of us to go stand on. God never says we are to stay only in safe places. The Good Samaritan acted compassionately. What he did was kind and loving. But it wasn't by any means safe.

Several times in my life and ministry, I've had to choose between safety and responding to God's call. At the top of this list is the decision I made in 1975 to move to Lawndale. A lot of people warned against it, but I sensed a call from God to do it. I found a nice little apartment, and my neighbors were kind to me. After about two weeks of being there, I invited some of the guys from the high school football team on which I was a coach to come over to my place for a Bible study. When I told them where I lived, they were shocked, because on my block was a tavern, known as "the bucket of blood," where a lot of violence occurred.

Several of the young men said they wouldn't go there. But a few of them were willing to put themselves in harm's way—to walk down a dangerous street or two—to come to my apartment for Bible study. Those young men bring to mind the remnant that God has used throughout history to accomplish His purposes. That Bible study sowed the seeds for everything we have today at Lawndale. Our church, our clinic, our development corporation, and all our other ministries—if those eight or ten hadn't come over, it could be that none of those things would be here today.

The Bible is full of accounts of faithful people living dangerously for God. The apostle Paul writes about being beaten—flogged to the point of being close to death. At various points in his ministry, he was stoned, beaten with rods, imprisoned, and shipwrecked. Despite the danger, he followed God's call.

After Anne and I married, we decided to live in the Lawndale neighborhood. During one period, our house got broken into three times in three days. Nobody was hurt, but we lost a lot of things. Someone stole my saw, my calculator, Anne's sewing machine, and our TV. After the third burglary, I was ready to throw in the towel and move somewhere else.

But the next morning, I began to read Scripture, and I came upon this passage where Paul was documenting all his travails. In 2 Corinthians 11:26, the word "danger" appears eight times. Paul wrote that he was in danger from rivers, danger from bandits, danger from natural forces, and even danger from his own people. I said to myself, "I haven't been beaten. Nobody has thrown any stones at me or whipped me. I lost a few things, but I'm okay. My wonderful wife, Anne, is okay." And I remember that morning, Anne and I recommitted our lives to what we felt God was calling us to do and to where God was calling us to be.

We need to come to terms with the fact that danger is a part of our faith. It comes with the territory. But we don't face that danger alone: "Whoever dwells in the shelter of the Most High will rest in the shadow of the Almighty. They say of the Lord, 'He is my refuge and my fortress, my God, in whom I trust'" (Psalm 91:1-2, *TNIV*).

It's not just the Bible that's full of danger stories. It's true of Christian history as well. Back in 1956, three graduates of Wheaton College, which is one of my alma maters, were among five missionaries, all in their 30s, who were killed because they chose faithfulness to God's calling over safety. While a student at Wheaton, I played football on McCully Field, named for Ed McCully, one of the five martyrs.

Ed, along with Jim Elliot, Nate Saint, Peter Fleming and Roger Youderian, was killed in Ecuador while attempting to share the love of Christ with the Auca Indians, a people group known for their violence. The missionaries had been dropping gifts for the Aucas from an airplane over a three-month period. Then they took the risk of meeting them in person. This story is captured in the 2006 film *The End of the Spear* and Elisabeth Elliot's book *Through Gates of Splendor*.

God's purposes were eventually accomplished among the Aucas. Jim Elliot's wife, Elisabeth, continued to reach out to the Auca Indians, as did Nate Saint's sister. And many in the tribe eventually came to Christ.

Keep in mind there is no place we can go that is totally safe. Jim Elliot once said that the safest place to be is at the center of God's will. Psalm 91 assures us that God will be our fortress, God's faithfulness our shield. We need not fear the terror of the night nor the arrows that fly by day, because our trust is in God. A thousand may fall at our side, but nothing will come near us unless God allows it.

And sometimes God does allow it. Sometimes when we take risks, we do get hurt. We pay a price. But keep in mind that though those five missionaries lost their lives, their souls are safe in God's hands. Our faith does not revolve around safety, nor does it grow if safety is our only concern. Rather, it is rooted in obedience and in sensitivity to God's leading. Where are the dangerous places God might be calling you to enter? Who are those people who might be dangerous to help? Remember, they are your neighbors.

36

My Neighbor Is Someone Who Is Discouraged

Although discouragement is certainly influenced by our circumstances, as I see it, it has a lot to do with attitude or state of mind. You probably know some people who have had to endure a lot of frustration and hardship, yet never seem to get discouraged. And then there are those on the opposite end of the spectrum—people who get discouraged the minute something, however small, goes wrong.

That said, who could blame the man who was beaten up and left on the side of the road for being discouraged? After all, he'd been severely injured and robbed of everything he had. He was helpless, and when two people who were in a position to help simply walked by, his hope—and his courage—began to disappear.

We all know what it's like to be discouraged. I doubt there is anyone who's not been discouraged about something. The person who lost his job and is having trouble finding another is discouraged, and sometimes it's hard not to let that discouragement show at the next job interview. I've known high school youth who are part of sports teams and get discouraged because they never miss practice and they work hard, but their coaches never put them in to play. Or they study hard for tests, but just can't seem to raise their grades.

People get discouraged when they tighten their belts as much as they can and still find too much month left at the end of the money. Or because they are not getting along with their bosses or with family members, and they don't know how to make things any different.

These are just a few of the many situations we face in life that bring about discouragement. To be discouraged is to be disheartened and deprived of hope. It's more than just being in a tough situation; it's not being able to conceive of things getting any better.

There's a family that lives just a few blocks from our church that at one point fit this description of discouragement precisely. The father in this family, Gino, earlier in his life, made some bad decisions, as many people do. He got involved in gang and drug activity and ended up in jail. While he was there, someone from a prison ministry led Gino to Christ.

He began getting his life back together. He eventually got married. He and his wife have six children, and Gino was doing his best to provide for them, but it wasn't easy. Instead of renting an apartment, he wanted his children to be able to live in a house, so he and his wife bought one. The problem was that, even though the house didn't cost a lot, Gino spent pretty much every nickel he had to buy it, and he had nothing left to fix it up with. The house was in total shambles. There were no working bathrooms, and the place was rat-infested. Gino, who felt responsible for providing for his family, got discouraged and was ready to give up.

I don't know how it happened, but someone from the TV show *Extreme Makeover: Home Edition* got wind of Gino's situation and decided to do something about it. The show's producers sent Gino and his family away for a week's vacation, and then several dozen workers—architects, electricians, painters and more—worked around the clock, totally redoing the house. They tore down the back wall and took off the roof, and they put in brand new windows, plumbing fixtures, and cabinets. Thousands of labor-hours and dollars went into this project. All of it was donated, including the architectural plans contributed by our church architects: McBride, Kelley and Bauer. Gino and his family came back to what might as well have been a brand new house. The workers even added a third floor, which included a music room for the kids.

I was fortunate enough to be on the scene—along with several other Lawndale Community Church people, including Joe, Stacy, Sarah and Jamila—when Gino and his family arrived back home. And what a scene it was when Ty yelled, "Move that bus!" Just like on TV. Nothing was staged. Gino, his wife, and their children were overcome with emotion. Their discouragement gave way to an overwhelming sense of gratitude and joy.

This joy was shared by those who had helped with the project, and also by observers, such as myself, who saw the whole thing unfold before our eyes. This was the gospel of Christ in action. Jesus calls us to put on our makeover hats and help those who are struggling, disheartened and discouraged.

Most of us are not able to do something as dramatic as helping to rebuild an entire house. But this should not stop us from doing what we can. Not far away from our church, there's a school at which the reading level of the students is less than half of the national norm. It's a tough place to teach. But a young woman from our church, Nikki, sensed a call from God to go there and teach sixth-grade boys.

Some people called her crazy, but Nikki moved into the neighborhood, right across the street from the school. She knew that what she was doing would be hard, but she also knew it was the right thing to do. Nikki has been very transparent with her church family about how much of a struggle it's been for her and about how, sometimes, she gets discouraged. She has stood up in church during prayer time, with tears streaming down her cheeks, and shared how hard it has been for her, partly because she loves these kids so much but sometimes sees little progress, and she knows how crucial it is for these young people to learn to read.

At one point, Nikki made contact with a college professor who gave her some advice. The professor said that for these young people to play chess or checkers was one way to develop their thinking skills, and it's something they enjoy doing. But Nikki couldn't play chess with all these boys at once. She needed volunteers to come in during school hours to help. The principal of the school gave his permission for men from Lawndale Community Church to come in. We challenged the men from our church to give just an hour or two during the week to this cause. And I'm glad to say that several responded. They came alongside a discouraged sister. So remember, sometimes it's not just people "out there" who need us. It's also people in ministry who have chosen to respond to the Lord's call, even though the path is tough.

Do you know someone who is discouraged? A father who's been out of work for a long time? A mother who is running out of the energy she needs to take care of her young children? A family caring for aging parents? Jesus helps us to see that our neighbors are people who are discouraged—who have begun to lose hope. Reach out to some such person today. Be a friend. Be their Good Samaritan. Bring them hope, and help to turn their discouragement into joy.

37

My Neighbor Is Someone Who Might Cost Me Money

In stopping to help the man who had been beaten and left on the side of the road, the Good Samaritan was likely risking his life and wellbeing. But one thing that often gets overlooked in this parable is that the Samaritan was also willing to help materially. That is, he was willing to spend some of his own money to help the man in need.

I suspect that, at least in pulpits across America, this gets overlooked because, even though money is mentioned many, many times in the Bible, most pastors are hesitant to talk about it. That's partly because most people in church don't want to hear about it. Some folks will come to church every Sunday, serve as an usher, sing in the choir, teach a Sunday School class, and even volunteer for nursery duty. But they don't want anyone talking about or asking for their money. That's where they draw the line.

Many pastors have come to dread Stewardship Sunday. They typically leave it up to someone else in the church—perhaps the chairman of the finance committee—to talk about money, especially when the financial news is not as positive as everyone would like it to be.

Be all that as it may, we cannot get around the fact that, among the several ways the Samaritan helped the man in need, one was to help him with his financial need. So if our goal is to become more faithful disciples of Christ, we can't simply sweep the topic of money under the proverbial rug, even if talking about it makes us feel a little uncomfortable.

Have you ever walked into the house of someone you don't know very well? And then begun to look around? You probably know that you can learn a lot about your host just by doing a bit of exploring. You can tell by the pictures on the wall if a couple has children, and by the presence or absence of trophies on the shelves, whether the kids are good at sports. You can see from the books or magazines on the coffee table what their interests might be. You can even learn a lot if you get a chance to look inside the trash can.

In a similar way, our bank statements and credit card bills reveal a lot about our interests and priorities. One person's credit card statement might show a purchase of tickets for a professional football game, while another's might reveal tickets to a concert or play. How we spend our money reflects our interests and values as people, and also as Christians. It's not possible to say that how we spend our money has nothing to do with our Christianity; the two are inextricably tied together.

As Christians, we are challenged to find the right balance between, on the one hand, enjoying the many good things God has given us and, on the other, not allowing material things to control our lives, dominate our priorities, and deprive us of the joy that comes from serving those whom Jesus called "the least of these."

The question that we must ask ourselves is, "Are we in control of our wealth or is our wealth—our stuff—in control of us?" Jesus says, "No one can serve two masters. Either you will hate the one and love the other, or you will be devoted to the one and despise the other. You cannot serve both God and Money" (Matthew 6:24, *TNIV*).

It's easy for people who live in a wealthy country with a capitalist economy to give in to the temptation of materialism. We're bombarded with television and billboard ads for fancy cars, five-star restaurants, and exquisite vacation resorts. We fall into the trap, no matter how much we have, of wanting more—a bigger house, a nicer car, the most fashionable clothes.

It has been well documented how Americans now typically spend money we don't have. We go into debt. There is research concluding that the number one deterrent to owning a home is a car payment. The car payment is so high that the prospective homebuyer can't afford to be making both a car payment and a house payment.

In previous generations, if someone wanted something, that person saved money until he or she had enough to buy the desired product. Nowadays, people seem to want everything they see, even if they don't really need it, can't afford it, or both. They don't have the discipline to say no. Some Christian authors have referred to the disease they call "affluenza," defined in terms of uncontrollable urges for greater affluence. By the time we get what we once thought would be enough, we no longer think it is enough. And the simple fact is that the more we give in to the disease of affluenza, the less we have to share with our neighbors, many of whom can't dream of owning any car or home, let alone nice ones.

The parable of the Good Samaritan has something important to teach us about money. In addition to helping his neighbor physically, the Samaritan covered his bill at the hotel. He started off by giving the hotel manager two denarii. Then he said if that wasn't enough, he was prepared to pay more. Now, "two denarii" doesn't sound like a lot until we realize that in those days, one denarius was equal to a full day's wages. So the Samaritan's first payment was the equivalent of someone today who makes $500 a week giving $200 of it to a stranger in need. Or someone who makes $1,000 a week giving $400. And that's just for starters. The point was abundantly clear to Jesus' original audience—as it should be to us— that the Samaritan was willing to make a financial sacrifice to demonstrate his love for his neighbor.

I know of a wealthy man who gave a good sum of money to a charitable organization. When someone from the organization visited the man to thank him, this donor said he wasn't satisfied with the amount he'd given. He wanted to make another gift. Explaining his reasons, he said, "The first gift wasn't enough to hurt." In other words, he wanted to give an amount that would require some sacrifice on his part.

This person understood the Bible's message about giving. It's not the dollar amount we give that matters most, but rather the level of sacrifice the gift represents. That's why Jesus praised the widow who gave just a small amount. She gave not out of her abundance, but out of genuine love.

We read in John's first epistle: "Jesus Christ laid down his life for us. And we ought to lay down our lives for one another. If any one of you has material possessions and sees a brother or sister in need but has no pity on them, how can the love of God be in you? Dear children, let us not love with words or tongue but with actions and in truth" (1 John 3:16-18, *TNIV*).

According to Scripture, those who cling to wealth—to material things—have their priorities way out of whack. Jesus said in the Sermon on the Mount, "Do not store up for yourselves treasures on earth, where moth and rust destroy, and where thieves break in and steal. But store up for yourselves treasures in heaven, where moth and rust do not destroy, and where thieves do not break in and steal. For where your treasure is, there will your heart be also" (Matthew 6:19-20). The Bible is clear that wealth has the potential to steer our hearts in the wrong direction.

If you want to get an idea of where your heart is, all you have to do is look at your credit card bill or bank statement. I challenge you to take a few months and keep close track of where your money goes. People I know who've done this are usually surprised at the results. You might think you don't eat out or buy new clothes as often as you do.

As many other churches do, we challenge the people at Lawndale to tithe, that is, to give 10 percent of their income to the church. I consider it giving to God's treasury. Ten percent ought to be the starting point. There are those who are able to give more and find joy in doing so. When it comes to giving 10 percent, we don't find it helpful to be legalistic or judgmental of others. We do encourage those who fall short to work at it harder. But we all need to be challenged. Just as we are challenged to improve in other areas of our Christian lives, we ought to be challenged when it comes to our material resources, since ultimately giving is a spiritual matter.

Barbara is a woman who lives in the Chicago suburbs and supports our church and its ministries. She helped pay for her children's and grandchildren's educations. She also was able to put some money aside for her retirement. She was in her 70s when she called the church and said she had a lot more money than she needed, and she wanted to help someone. Specifically, she wanted to put somebody else through college.

So we found a person who was struggling with finances, and this woman provided a scholarship to pay for an entire college education, including books, room and board. After that person graduated, Barbara said she wanted to do the same thing for another student. By my calculation, she gave about $20,000 per person per year to help two young people get a college education debt-free.

I hope that we can all be inspired by the examples of people who share their material wealth with their neighbors instead of giving in to the temptation to get bigger and better things.

38

My Neighbor Is in Need of Tender Loving Care

It may seem like a fine distinction, but I like to distinguish between showing another person love and showing that person some tender loving care, or TLC. We demonstrate love for another when we do something or say something that helps that person in some way. Helping a family fix up a house, buying a homeless person a meal, and giving money to a worthy cause are examples of love. To me, tender loving care implies a kind of love that in some way is a bit more personal, more thoughtful, and more—as the name implies—tender.

Let me give you an example. I know of a family who had a child who was severely deformed. The parents, especially the mother, had to care not only for this infant child but also for a toddler. People from their church pitched in and helped in many different ways, including providing meals for the first several weeks. But one of the best gifts this family received was, of all things, a batch of chocolate chip cookies. It was a special gift because the family who "donated" the cookies didn't just bake them and drop them off. Instead, they mixed up the batter, brought it over to the house, and baked the cookies there. Their reasoning was that a big part of enjoying chocolate chip cookies is experiencing the smell of them baking in the oven and then being able to eat at least a few of them while they are still warm and the chips are soft and gooey.

This may seem like a small thing. (A cookie is a cookie, right?) But that's the essence of tender loving care. It consists of small, subtle acts of kindness that demonstrate going the extra mile in terms of thoughtfulness. To the family that received those cookies, the message was not just, "We're giving you some cookies tonight." Rather, it was, "We're thinking of every possible way we can show you we care, even in the small things, like wanting you to enjoy the aroma of cookies baking in the oven."

The man who was beaten up and left on the side of the road was in need of many things. But one of the things the Good Samaritan provided was some tender loving care. He could have just put the injured man on his donkey and taken him to where he could get help, which would have been a good and loving thing to do. But he also took the time to bandage the man's wounds and to "pour on oil and wine," which I suspect was a first-century way to cleanse the wounds as painlessly as possible.

It's not hard for me to imagine that the Good Samaritan's touch was soft and gentle as he bandaged the beaten man's wounds. He probably was as careful as he could be to inflict as little pain as possible. In other words, he showed some tender loving care.

When I think of TLC, again I think not of the big, obvious things but of the small things that most people wouldn't think of. I'm reminded of Paul's admonition: "Be kind and compassionate to one another, forgiving each other, just as in Christ God forgave you. Follow God's example, therefore, as dearly loved children and walk in the way of love, just as Christ loved us and gave himself up for us as a fragrant offering and sacrifice to God" (Ephesians 4:32-5:2, *TNIV*).

I've mentioned elsewhere that loving our neighbors might sometimes require some sacrifice of time, money or both. Not so with tender loving care. All that it requires is a little extra thoughtfulness, rooted in kindness and compassion.

A simple word of encouragement can demonstrate TLC, and words are free. All of us can probably point to times in our lives when someone said something to us that was so encouraging and uplifting that we've never forgotten it. I hope you will look for opportunities to bless others in a similar way. In the course of a day or week, most likely you will run across at least one other person who needs to hear an encouraging word. Be the person who delivers such a word. Say something that shows you have been paying close attention. Let your neighbor see that you care.

Often, what somebody needs along the path of life isn't something big that requires a lot of time and sacrifice. They don't need how-to books or lectures that address all the mistakes they've made and provide instructions for how to fix them. They just need somebody to come alongside them for a while and show them some tender loving care.

I urge you to think about the kind of thoughtfulness that went into the gift of chocolate chip cookies mentioned above. Then show some similar tender loving care to a neighbor. Do something or say something you could not possibly have done or said unless you were paying close attention. Chances are that neighbor will remember your kindness forever.

39

My Neighbor Is Someone Who Feels Defeated

In almost every sporting event, there are winners and losers. Not too many competitions end in a draw anymore. Our culture doesn't like ties. It used to be that a college football game could end in a tie. Now they go to overtime and play until there's a winner. It's the same thing with professional hockey. If neither team wins in the overtime period, they go to a shootout. And the shootout keeps on going until somebody finally wins.

You might say that the man who was beaten and left to die on the side of the road was forced to engage in a series of competitions. And he lost all of them. He lost the battle to hold on to his money. He lost the battle to get to whatever destination he was trying to reach. In his efforts to hold on to his clothes, he was defeated. Assuming that he tried to defend himself as a boxer would, he lost that contest as well. Except for the fact that he was able to stay alive, he was totally defeated.

As we think about the people around us who may be defeated, it's important to distinguish between merely losing and being defeated. A sports team can lose a game, but not be defeated. The players and coaches simply put the loss behind them and start thinking about the next game. A team can lose most of its games—maybe even all of its games—and still not be defeated. They escape defeat by maintaining a positive outlook and by never giving up, regardless of their record. A team is defeated not when it loses a game, but when it loses the will to win. It's defeated when it quits trying—when it gives up the fight.

The same principle applies to other arenas in life. I've heard it said that a good salesperson and a not-so-good salesperson get the same number of rejections. And in fact, for most salespersons, the overwhelming majority of sales calls end in rejection. The difference between good and not so good is that the good salesperson, after getting 10 rejections in a row, still believes he'll strike gold on the eleventh call, whereas the not-so-good salesperson is ready to give up after the fourth or fifth rejection.

Losing involves being disappointed in a particular outcome. But being defeated goes well beyond that. To be defeated is to have the life and the will to go on sucked out of us to the point where we just want to throw in the towel and give up the fight. There are dozens of situations in life that can cause us to feel defeated. Many of them have been mentioned earlier in this book. People can feel defeated in their marriages when the same problems keep cropping up. The husband and wife have the same arguments time and time again. Neither gives in. Neither person wins. Both feel defeated.

I suspect that anyone who has ever had a teenage son or daughter knows what it's like to feel defeated. I saw a sign once that read, "Hurry up and hire a teenager while he still knows everything!" The truth is that it's virtually impossible for a teen to understand the parent's perspective, and it's probably just as hard for most parents to remember what it was like to be a teenager or to understand how things are different today. And so a tug of war ensues, and we feel like giving up. We feel defeated.

Some people feel defeated after having tried and failed to give up a bad habit or to overcome some kind of addiction. You've probably heard the quip: "It's easy to stop smoking. I know because I've done it many times." People, including sincere Christians, struggle to overcome addictions to tobacco products, illegal drugs, and alcohol. Others feel enslaved to pornography. Now we're beginning to hear about people who are addicted to Facebook. Often people make an effort to overcome whatever they are addicted to. They succeed for a while, but then something happens that triggers some old emotion, and pretty soon they're back to where they were. Feeling defeated. If we try and fail enough times, it's hard not to feel defeated.

It's often difficult to know how to help or what to say to someone who feels defeated. It's usually not enough to say, "Just stay positive. Everything's gonna be all right." It's not that simple. We don't know what kinds of emotional resources these defeated persons received from the families in which they were reared. Perhaps they didn't get anywhere close to what they needed emotionally, and they are still struggling as a result. Nor do we know what kinds of life experiences, including repeated failures, may have chipped away over the years at whatever resources they have, or had at one time. What we *do* know is that these people who feel defeated are our neighbors.

We can find at various points in Scripture admonitions to show care and concern for people who feel defeated. For some of these people, their resources have become so depleted they are no longer able to fend for themselves. As we've seen, Proverbs 31 issues a challenge for the stronger among us to speak up for those who cannot speak for themselves, who've been defeated, and who've had their energy and will to go on sucked out of them. In Acts 9, we read about a disciple named Dorcas, a woman who the Bible says "was always doing good and helping the poor," apparently by, among other things, making clothing.

In 1 Timothy 5, Paul instructs widows to devote themselves to good deeds, such as showing hospitality, washing the feet of the Lord's people, and helping those in trouble. Scripture is full of passages that speak to how we, as believers, even if we have suffered our own losses, are to look for people who feel defeated and choose to walk alongside of them—as Dorcas did, and as Jesus Himself did.

We are surrounded by people who feel defeated in their life circumstances. It could be that they were just evicted from their apartment, or their home is in foreclosure. They may have lost their job—been fired, or been laid off in a downsizing. It may be a defeat in a personal relationship—a painful divorce or the death of a child. For a young person who has not done well in school, failing a class or having to repeat a grade indicates defeat. These are just some of the defeats people around us face on a daily basis. These defeated people are our neighbors.

To use the metaphor cited in an earlier chapter, the buckets of defeated people are empty, or almost empty. And it's our job as believers to refill them. In so doing, we fill our own buckets as well. We may not have the resources or the ability to give people everything they need. For example, if they need a job, we might not know of a place that is hiring. We certainly can't do much to replace the love they may not have received earlier in life. But don't underestimate the value of seemingly little things. An encouraging word, a card or note, a smile, a hug, a high-five, or simply checking in on them unexpectedly can go a long way toward communicating to such persons that someone cares, that somebody loves them. No gesture of kindness is too small or insignificant. So notice those persons around you who are feeling defeated. It might be a son or daughter, a parent, or a co-worker. Show them that you care. Consider it not just your responsibility as a follower of Christ, but a privilege, too.

40

My Neighbor Is Someone I Am Able to Help

The man who was beaten and left on the side of the road was eminently helpable. His problem was not some theoretical or imaginary issue with an uncertain or indefinite solution. Plain and simple, he needed help, and that was clear to anyone who passed by and saw him. The priest who came by could have stopped and helped. He chose not to. Next came a Levite, who was also in a position to help. He likewise chose not to do anything.

Nothing about the situation had changed by the time the Good Samaritan arrived. If anything, the beaten man was in worse shape. But the pros and cons associated with helping or not helping were the same. The Samaritan simply made a different choice. He chose to stop. He knew what he needed to do to help, and he did it.

When I state that our neighbors are helpable, I do so with the realization that not all people are helpable all the time. That is, there are situations where, no matter how much we care and would like to help, we are not in a position to do so. There are people all over the world—and right in our backyards—whom we may not be able to help. We might not have the material resources or the ability or the knowledge that the situation requires.

Sometimes, we're just not in the right place at the right time. I recall on one occasion being in Washington, DC, to meet with some members of Congress on issues related to poverty. It was February, and back in Chicago it was one of those cold, below-zero days—one of the coldest days of the year. My wife, Anne, was heading off to work at the preschool where she teaches. Her car stalled while she was driving on the Eisenhower Expressway, one of the busiest expressways in the Chicago area.

When Anne called to tell me her car had broken down, I was in the Senate office building. I felt terrible about Anne's situation. I wished it had been me in a rough spot instead of her. But the reality was that, no matter how much I cared, there was nothing I could possibly do to help her in that situation. For me, in that particular moment, Anne was simply not helpable. (I mention as an aside that a "Good Samaritan" did stop and help Anne. By God's providence, Richard, one of the leaders of our church, recognized Anne and her car, stopped, invited Anne to sit in his warm car until the tow truck arrived, and then drove Anne back to our house so she could take my car to work.)

It's important for us to recognize and accept that there will be times when we are not able to help. But it's also important not to allow this recognition to overwhelm us and to keep us from acting on the opportunities we do have. I've stated it earlier, but it's important to note that, sometimes, because we can't solve all the world's problems, we get discouraged and give up. We fail to notice the situations in which those who need help are helpable. In summary, my neighbors are those whom I have both the opportunity and the ability to help.

I hope that the reflections, ideas and stories in this book have made you more sensitive to people in need, more observant, and more capable of recognizing the neighbors that surround you.

And I hope you have been challenged to pursue the opportunities you have to help those neighbors.

It all starts with Jesus and our striving to understand Him and be more like Him. "Come to Me, all who are weary and heavy-laden," He said, "and I will give you rest" (Matthew 11:28, *NASB*). When He walked on the earth, Jesus reached out to those who were experiencing various kinds of pain or discrimination. He healed the sick and gave sight to the blind. He met with sinners and told them they could make a brand new start. He made sure that tax collectors knew He loved them even if no one else did.

Most of us are surrounded by helpable people every day of our lives. If nothing else, we can help in small ways. Open the door for other people. Help an elderly person carry grocery bags or volunteer to go shopping for her. Keep jumper cables in your car so you're prepared to help someone who has car trouble. People will understand if you're a few minutes late to your meeting, especially if you tell them why you were delayed. As noted earlier, one simple and cost-free way of reaching out to a neighbor is by offering comforting or encouraging words.

These are not the kinds of things that will land you on the six o'clock news. But as you become more sensitive to the neighbors around you, your striving to emulate the Good Samaritan can lead to other things. Perhaps you'll be moved to take a homeless person to lunch instead of just ignoring him or giving him a few bucks to spend on who knows what. Perhaps you'll become a tutor for high school kids struggling to learn to read. Or a father figure to a boy who doesn't know who his father is. Maybe God will move you to visit prisoners and help them turn their lives around. Maybe God will move you to take even greater risks, as suggested by the words of John: "This is how we know what love is: Jesus Christ laid down his life for us. And we ought to lay down our lives for one another" (1 John 3:16, *TNIV*). Our neighbors are not just the people who live next door to us, who look like us, who have been educated like us, who have the same lifestyle as us, or who come from the same race as us. No, our neighbors are people like the man who was beaten up and left on the side of the road.

As we conclude, I want to leave you with two final thoughts. First, I want you to think about striving to become the kind of person who stops. The priest didn't stop. The Levite didn't stop. Will you stop? The reality is that, if we never stop, our love, in keeping with the words of 1 Corinthians 13, is nothing more than a loud, clanging cymbal. So my plea is that you will be the kind of person— the kind of Christ follower—who stops to help your neighbor.

Finally, trust me when I say that there is great joy in stopping. I am quite sure the Good Samaritan had no regrets. Maybe he was late for his appointment. Maybe he was short of cash for a while because of what he spent on his neighbor. But nothing can replace the joy we experience when we overcome our fears and hesitations, and stop to help a neighbor in need. As you notice the neighbors around you—and stop to help them—God will bless you in ways you cannot imagine. My prayer for you is that God will bring you great joy as you ask, "Who is my neighbor?" and as you find answers and opportunities all around you.

Let us all obey our Lord Jesus Christ's command and "LOVE OUR NEIGHBORS AS WE LOVE OURSELVES"!

THE EIGHT COMPONENTS
OF CHRISTIAN COMMUNITY
DEVELOPMENT

Nehemiah begins with lamenting over the city of Jerusalem: "Those who survived the exile and are back in the province are in great trouble and disgrace. The wall of Jerusalem is broken down, and its gates have been burned with fire" (Neh. 1:3, *NIV*).

This describes the situation in parts of most American cities today. They have been neglected and allowed to deteriorate for almost 40 years. The Church of Jesus Christ has at best sat back and watched this happen, yet in many areas has contributed to the problem. The words of Nehemiah, "great trouble and disgrace," ring true for us in the Church today.

The question arises as to what the response of Christians will be to the troubles of the poor and the inner cities today. The desperate conditions that face the poor call for a revolution in the Church's attempts at a solution. Through years of experience among the poor, many have come to see that these desperate problems cannot be solved without strong commitment, heroic faith and risky actions on the parts of ordinary Christians.

There are many philosophies that seek to solve the problems of the poor, but most fall short of any lasting change. The most creative long-term solutions to the problems of the poor are coming from grass-roots and church-based efforts. The solutions are coming from people who see themselves as the replacements, the agents, for Jesus here on Earth, in their own neighborhoods and communities.

Those who see themselves as Christ's agents have formed a philosophy that is known as Christian Community Development. This philosophy is not a concept developed in a classroom, nor is it formulated by people foreign to the poor community. These are biblical, practical principles evolved from years of living and working among the poor.

John Perkins, in Mississippi, first developed this philosophy. John and Vera Mae Perkins moved back to their homeland of Mississippi from California in 1960 to help alleviate poverty and oppression. Through their work and ministry, Christian Community Development was conceived. Christian Community Development has a proven track record with over 600 models around the country that are making great progress in difficult communities.

The Eight Components

Christian Community Development has eight essential components that have evolved over the last 40 years. The first three are based on John Perkins's Three *R*s of community development: relocation, reconciliation and redistribution. The rest have been developed by many Christians who are working together to find ways to rebuild poor neighborhoods. The following is a brief description of the eight key components to Christian Community Development.

Relocation: Living Among the People

Living out the gospel means desiring the same thing for your neighbor and neighbor's family as that which you desire for yourself and your family. Living out the gospel means bettering the quality of other people's lives spiritually, physically, socially and emotionally as you better your own life. Living out the gospel means sharing in the suffering and pain of others.

A key phrase to understanding relocation is "incarnational ministry." How did Jesus love? "The Word became flesh and dwelt among us, and we beheld His glory, the glory as of the only begotten of the Father, full of grace and truth" (John 1:14). Jesus relocated. He became one of us. He didn't commute back and forth to heaven. Similarly, the most effective messenger of the gospel to the poor will also live among those to whom God has called that person.

Relocation is community-based in the very essence of the word. There are three kinds of people who live in the community. First, "relocators" are people who were not born in the inner city but moved into the neighborhood. Second are the "returners." These are the people born and raised in their community who then left for a better life. Usually they return from college or the military. They are no longer trapped by the surrounding poverty of their neighborhood. Yet, they choose to return and live in the community they once tried to escape. Last are the "remainers." These are the ones that could have fled the problems of the inner city but chose to stay and be part of the solution to the problems surrounding them.

By relocating, a person will understand most clearly the real problems facing the poor and then he or she may begin to look for real solutions. For example, if a person ministering in a poor community has children, one can be sure that person will do everything possible to ensure that the children of the community get a good education. Relocation transforms "you, them and theirs" to "we, us and ours." Effective ministries plant and build communities of believers that have a personal stake in the development of their neighborhoods.

There is no question that relocation is the linchpin of Christian Community Development and that all other principles of development draw on it for meaning.

Reconciliation

Reconciling People to God. Reconciliation is at the heart of the gospel. Jesus said that the essence of Christianity could be summed up in two inseparable commandments: Love God and love thy neighbor (see Matt. 22:37-39). First, then, Christian Community Development is concerned with reconciling people to God and bringing them into a church fellowship where they can be discipled in their faith.

Evangelism is very much a part of Christian Community Development. The answer to community development is not just providing a job or a decent place to live, but it is also having a true relationship with Jesus Christ. It is essential that the good news of Jesus Christ is proclaimed and that individuals place their faith in Him for salvation.

The gospel, rightly understood, is "wholistic." It responds to people as whole people; it does not single out just spiritual or just physical needs and speak to those. Christian Community Development begins with people being transformed by the love of God, who then respond to God's call to share the gospel with others through evangelism, social action, economic development and justice.

Reconciling People to People. The most racially segregated time of the week in our nation is Sunday morning during church services. At church, Christians often pray the model prayer that the Lord taught: "Your kingdom come, your will be done on earth as it is in heaven" (Matt. 6:10, *NIV*). This prayer teaches that churches should reflect heaven on Earth—and heaven will be the most integrated place in the world. People of every nation and every tongue will worship Christ together. This is the picture of the Church that Christ presents to His people. American churches, however, are rarely integrated and thus weaken the gospel because of this practice.

The question that we're left with, then, is, Can a gospel that reconciles people to God without reconciling people to people be the true gospel of Jesus Christ? A person's love for Christ should break down every racial, ethnic and economic barrier in a united effort to solve the problems of the community. For example, Christian Community Development recognizes that the entire Body of Christ—black, white, brown and yellow; rich and poor; urban and suburban; educated and uneducated—needs to share the task of loving the poor.

While the Bible transcends culture and race, the Church is still having a hard time with living out the reality of unity in Christ. Christian Community Development, on the other hand, is intentional about reconciliation and works hard to bring people of all races and cultures into the one worshiping Body of Christ. This comes not so much through a program but through a commitment to living together in the same neighborhood. This is why relocation is so important.

This is also where what Dr. John Perkins calls the *felt-need concept* can be so helpful for individuals who are seeking to establish authentic cross-cultural relationships in under-resourced neighborhoods. In order to build trust with people who may be suspicious about our motives for being in the "hood" because of negative past experiences, stereotypes or ignorance, we must begin by getting to know people right where they are. As we listen to their stories and get to know their hopes and concerns for the present and future, we also begin to identify the community's deepest felt-needs: those hurts and longings that allow us opportunities to connect with people on a deeper level, which is always necessary for true reconciliation to take place.

The power of authentic reconciliation between God and us, and between people of every culture and race is an essential component of effective ministry in our hurting world.

Redistribution (Just Distribution of Resources)

When men and women in the Body of Christ are visibly present and living among the poor (relocation), and when people are intentionally loving their neighbors and their neighbors' families as their own (reconciliation), the result is redistribution, or a just distribution of resources. When God's people who have resources (regardless of their race or culture) commit to living in underserved communities, seeking to be good neighbors, being examples of what it means to be a follower of Christ, working for justice for the entire community, and utilizing their skills and resources to address the problems of that community alongside their neighbors, then redistribution is being practiced.

Redistribution brings the principles of justice back to the underserved communities. Justice has left communities of color and lower economic status, leaving an unjust criminal court and prison system, unjust hiring practices, unjust housing development, and injustice in the educational institutions. Justice has been available only to people with the economic means to acquire just treatment.

Redistribution, though, brings new skills, new relationships and new resources and puts them to work to empower the residents of a given community to bring about healthy transformation. This is redistribution: when Christian Community Development ministries harness the commitment and energy of men, women and young people living in the community, and others who care about their community, and find creative avenues to develop jobs, schools, health centers, home ownership opportunities and other enterprises of long-term development.

Seeking a just distribution of resources and working for justice in underserved communities contribute greatly to helping people help themselves, which is at the heart of Christian Community Development.

Leadership Development

The primary goal of leadership development is to develop leaders in order to restore the stabilizing glue and fill the vacuum of moral, spiritual and economic leadership that is so prevalent in poor communities. This is accomplished most effectively by raising up Christian leaders from the community of need who will remain in the community to live and lead. Most Christian Community Development ministries put a major focus on youth development, winning youth to Christ as early as kindergarten and then following them all the way through college with spiritual and educational nurturing. Upon returning to the community from college, a ministry creates opportunities for those former students to exercise leadership.

At the core of the leadership vacuum in inner-city communities is an attitude of flight. For many, success is defined as being able to move out of inner-city communities, to own a home in a more affluent area. The erroneous goal is to help a few people leave the neighborhood so that they can escape the problems of inner-city communities. But this core value of escapism has caused a major drain on inner-city communities.

There is a drain on leadership development because it is possible only when there is longevity of ministry. All too often people are guilty of trying to have quick fixes in poor neighborhoods. For example, since leadership development is of the highest priority in Christian Community Development, each ministry must have a dynamic youth ministry. And each youth ministry must be reaching young people with the good news of Jesus Christ and then equipping them to become faithful followers of Christ and effective community leaders. This will take at least 15 years to accomplish, so a worker must plan to stay in the neighborhood for at least that long.

In situations where Latinos and other ethnic groups are negatively affected by their current legal status in our country, this progressive, developmental process is nearly impossible to accomplish, as young people are not able to attend college or prepare for a stable career. In this case, ministries are often moved to engage in social action to challenge and change current immigration laws that debilitate the lives of promising youths and their families.

For CCD ministries, developing leaders from the community is a huge priority that requires absolute commitment. The payoff is that our communities will be filled with strong Christian leaders who love their neighbors and have the skills and abilities to lead our churches, organizations and other institutions to bring sustainable health to our communities.

Listening to Community

Often communities are developed by people from the outside who bring in resources without taking into account the community itself. Christian Community Development, however, is committed to listening to the community residents and hearing their dreams, ideas and thoughts. This is often referred to as the *felt need concept*. Listening is most important, as the people of the community are the vested treasures of the future.

It is important not to focus on the weaknesses or needs of a community. Again, the felt need concept, as referred to above, helps us as community developers to focus on the desires of the community residents. The priority is the thoughts and dreams of the community itself—what the people themselves believe should be the focus. Asset-based community development focuses on the assets of a community and builds upon them. When felt needs are fused together with community assets through Christian Community Development, this can have extremely positive results.

Every community has assets that are often neglected. When a ministry utilizes *Asset-Based Community Development* (ABCD), it names all of the assets in the community that help the community see its many positive characteristics. It is through these assets that people develop their community.

Christian Community Development realistically points out, through community meetings and efforts, some of the areas that people in the community would like to see improved. The areas to be focused on are not looked at from some outside group or demographic study that is laid upon the community. Instead, it is the community members themselves who decide what areas they would like to improve.

After a community has decided where it wants to focus some of its attention, it is then directed to the means with which it can bring this about. What qualities, talents and abilities does the community have that can help solve these problems? The focus is on the community members seeing themselves as the solution to the problem, not some government program or outside group that is going to be their salvation.

It is essential for community leaders to help the community focus on maximizing their strengths and abilities to make a difference for their community. The philosophy of Christian Community Development believes that the people with the problems have the best solutions and opportunities to solve those problems. Christian Community Development, then, affirms the dignity of individuals and encourages the engagement of the community to use its own resources and assets to bring about sustainable change.

Church-based Community Development
Nothing other than the community of God's people is capable of affirming the dignity of the poor and enabling them to meet their own needs. It is practically impossible to do effective wholistic ministry apart from the local church. A nurturing community of faith can best provide the thrusts of evangelism, discipleship, spiritual accountability and relationships by which disciples grow in their walk with God.

One problem today, however, has been that the Church is not involved in developing its communities. Often, the Church has been an unfriendly neighbor in communities across our country. Churches are guilty of being open only on Sunday mornings and Wednesday nights and being almost irrelevant to the needs of the people around them. Because of this, many parachurch organizations have started to do the work of loving their neighbors that the Church has neglected.

Christian Community Development, in contrast, sees the Church as taking action toward the development of its community. It is the responsibility of the Church to evangelize, disciple and nurture people in the Kingdom. Yet, from the command of Jesus, it is also the responsibility of the Church to love their neighbor and their neighborhood. Churches, then, should be seen as lovers of their communities and neighborhoods.

As community and neighborhood lovers, it is out of the Church body that ideas and programs that bolster community life should emerge. This concept is certainly not new in the black community. The black Church has spawned most of the substantial community efforts in housing and economic development. There have been shopping centers built, senior housing units developed and communities transformed by the Church. As natural as these transformations have been for the black Church (also, recently many new efforts are emerging in the Latino and Asian communities that are making the Church even more relevant to those they serve), they continue to be foreign to the traditional white Church. Often, opposition to the Church's involvement in community development still occurs among many white denominations and Church groups.

Finally, probably the greatest sustaining power of community development is the presence of a local church. Because Christian Community Development is based on relocation and people living in the community, having a local church in which to worship together is essential. It is in the church where people gather to be rejuvenated and have their personal needs met. This is true of staff members and non-staff members. How exciting it is to see doctors at a local health center worshiping and sitting next to their patients on a Sunday morning. This is community building at its best.

The church helps people to understand that each person has gifts and talents and that all must utilize those for the greater good of the community. And a worshiping church breaks down many of the barriers, including racial, educational and cultural barriers, that often separate people in communities.

A Wholistic Approach

Often, many in ministry get passionate and involved in one area of need and think that if they solve that one particular problem that all else will be resolved. Christians, of course, often focus this area on a personal relationship with Jesus Christ. Certainly, the most essential elements to Christian Community Development are evangelism and discipleship. Yet solving problems with lasting solutions requires more.

There is never a simplistic answer to the problems in poor communities. Often, people will say that the problem is spiritual, social or educational. These are problems, but they are only part of the larger problems. Solving the housing problem does not solve the emotional struggles that a person has. Christian Community Development, though, has a wholistic approach to ministry that deals with the spiritual, social, economic, political, cultural, emotional, physical, moral, judicial, educational and familial issues of each person.

The wholistic approach is difficult because there are so many aspects to a person's life. That is why there is no better way of helping a person than having him or her committed to a local church. A church that is committed to Christian Community Development sees not only the soul of a person as significant but also his or her whole life on earth. It is being completely pro-life for a person, not only eternally, but also as the person lives on this earth.

Therefore, Christian Community Development sees that the Church must be involved in every aspect of a person's life. In order to accomplish the wholistic aspect of ministry, pastors and leaders must be networkers. Christian Community Development builds coalitions in communities so that they can work together to solve the problems.

Empowerment

Empowering people as community developers to meet their needs is an important element to Christian Community Development. How does a pastor ensure that people are able to help themselves after they have been helped? Often Christian ministry, particularly in poor communities, creates dependency. This is no better than the federal government welfare program. But the Bible teaches empowerment, not dependency.

In the Old Testament, empowerment is an important aspect to God's care for the poor. In Deuteronomy 24 and Leviticus 19, God instituted the gleaning system. The farmers harvested their crops but were only allowed to go through the field one time. What was left behind or dropped on the ground was available for any widow, alien, orphan or poor person to come and harvest. Thus, this program was one that empowered people.

Three principles come out of God's welfare system in the Old Testament. First, there must be opportunity for people to get their needs met. In Deuteronomy and Leviticus, this happened to be a field with food in it. Second, the person who has a need must be willing to work for it. The widow, alien, orphan or poor person had to go into the field and pick up the crops which, then, involved work on the part of the poor. This is also found in 2 Thessalonians 3:10, which says that if you don't work, you don't eat. Third, when these first two principles are working, a person's dignity is affirmed. All people have inherited dignity because we were all created in the image of God. Oftentimes, charity demeans a person and strips him or her of dignity. In contrast, the last principle of empowerment affirms a person's God-given dignity.

Track Record

There are over 600 organizations in over 200 cities and 40 states practicing Christian Community Development. These churches and ministries are showing that it is possible that the Church can live out the love of God in the world; that black and white and yellow and brown, rich and poor together, can be reconciled; that we can make a difference; that we can rescue the ghettoes and barrios of this nation.

In these hundreds of communities and cities across the world, these defining principles of Christian Community Development are proving that grass-roots, community-based ministries led by people who have made the community their own are the most effective agents for healing the poor.

The following poem is used as a philosophical guide to those working on Christian Community Development:

Go to the people
Live among them
Learn from them
Love them
Start with what they know
Build on what they have:
But of the best leaders
When their task is done
The people will remark
"We have done it ourselves."

Conclusion

Clearly there are great needs in neglected inner-city communities throughout our nation. There is a lack of leadership in these communities, and it is essential that new leadership be developed from among the people. These communities face a variety of cultural and environmental factors that impact the health of these neighborhoods. Thus, Christian Community Development, I believe, represents the best approach to not only develop these future leaders but also to transform our most under-resourced communities into thriving communities through the power of God and the efforts of His people.

APPRECIATION

Whenever a person endeavors to write a book like this there are dozens of people who deserve credit and appreciation.

First and foremost, thanks goes to my family. We are close-knit; we love each other and do life together. Thanks to Anne, my wife of 33 years, who has walked with me through this book and life itself. She, most importantly, has taught me how to love my neighbor by her loving people. She really has the gift of friendship and is a friend to many, including me.

Thanks to Angela, my daughter and committed educator. She has gotten her Masters degree in early childhood education and is applying it in a school here in Lawndale. Angela has a special gift in working with children. She has committed her life to helping children in the inner city. My daughter, Angela, has a place in my heart that is immeasurable; she is my special girl.

Thanks to Andrew, my oldest son and good friend. Andrew and I try to have breakfast together every Saturday morning when we discuss the deep issues of life. Andrew is our deep thinker and challenges me to think beyond the surface. He has had lots of insights and ideas concerning loving your neighbor for years. Since Andrew was a young boy he has been able to discern effective ways to help people without causing them to feel badly about themselves.

Thanks to Austin, my youngest child. Austin has probably traveled with me the most of any of our children. At the age of 4 he was with me speaking in Detroit. He gave a little speech that summed up the concept of loving our neighbors: "My dad and I drive around our community and look for houses that have broken windows. Our church buys them. Then we help people fix them up and then they live in them." What more can we say. Austin continues to care about the hurting people of our world.

Stacy was a gift to our family in 2007 when she and our son Andrew got married. Stacy is a blessing to all of us and has her own special gift of helping people feel good about themselves. She loves life and loves people.

Thanks to those who have worked with me and become part of my extended family. Joe and Stacy Atkins, who along with their family have taught all of us how to be good neighbors. Both are indigenous leaders in our community, demonstrating a love for all people. Joe was one of the high school young people who founded Lawndale Community Church and is now my associate pastor.

Thanks to Bruce Miller, the CEO of Lawndale Christian Health Center, which strives to love God and love people every day by providing quality affordable health care in an atmosphere of Christian love.

Thanks to Kim Jackson, the executive director of Lawndale Christian Development Corporation. LCDC is involved in providing affordable and quality housing for our community. Also LCDC is striving to empower the people of Lawndale through education, economic development and community organizing.

Thanks to my accountability group that meets monthly, holding me accountable to my work of faith and encouraging me: Noel Castellanos, Alex duBuclet, Marshall Hatch, Vance Henry, Hutz Hertzberg and Bob Muzikowski.

Thanks to Phil Jackson, pastor of our hip-hop church, The House. His creative love for young people is an example to me.

Thanks to the staff of Lawndale Community Church, who have been involved daily with me in creatively loving our neighbors. Our staff has worked tirelessly to love the people of Lawndale who are our neighbors. Current staff of LCC: Joseph Atkins, Antoine Allen, Darrin Brown, Charles "Bo" Delaney, Terence Gadsden, Angela Gordon, Willette Grant, Victor Heard, Phil Jackson, Chelsea Johnson, Linda Johnson, Linda Jones, Jason Little, Pam McCain, Carrie Moore, Cliff Nellis, Wardell Tate, Stanley Ratliff, Marvin Rowe, Darryl Saffore, Theo Thompson, Sarah Torenga, Jesse Warfield.

Thanks to Chelsea Johnson, Willette Grant and Charisse Dower for helping to transcribe this original manuscript.

Thanks to our boards at Lawndale Community Church, the members of which have been an encouragement to me over the years, counseling and guiding all of our attempts to love our neighbors. Current board members of LCC: Jerry Bolden, Janet Ford, Adonya Little, Kathryn Miller, Anthony Pegues, Freddie Simmons, Dave Wilcoxen, Thomas Worthy, Sheila Avery, Perry Bigelow, Randy Brown, Tanesha Daniels, Donnie Graham, Andrew Moore, Barbara Rice, Floyd Richardson, Stephanie Townsell and Lisa Wilcoxen.

Thanks to John M. Perkins who began as my hero in 1975 when I heard him speak in chapel at Wheaton College. John has continued to have a profound impact on my life, becoming my role model for ministry, teaching me the concept of Christian Community Development. He is my mentor, then my co-laborer in Christian Community Development and now one of my best friends in life. We talk on the phone almost every day and John continues to build into my life. He has also been a major part of the Gordon family and has a very close relationship with Anne and all of our children.

Thanks to the CCDA board. All of us in CCDA continue to walk with each other and do life together. Our board meetings are full of both tears and laughter. Current CCDA board members: Andy Bales, Leroy Barber, John Booy, Crissy Brooks, Delia Caderno, Luis A. Carlo, Kit Danley, Gerald Davis, Alex duBuclet, Paul Green, Joe Holland, Chris Jehle, Tammi Jehle, Glen Kehrein, John Liotti, Robert Lupton, Mayra Macedo-Nolan, Mary Nelson, John Perkins, Patty Prasada-Rao, Soong-Chan Rah, Alvin Sanders, Harold Spooner, Arloa Sutter, Jim Swearingen, Ted Travis, Matthew Watts and Barbara Williams-Skinner.

Thanks to all the people of Lawndale Community Church who have walked with me for 32 years. Together we have tried to live out these chapters and to love God and to love people. The people of Lawndale are so amazing; Anne and I are so blessed to have deep personal relationships with so many in our church body. What a privilege to pastor a church that is striving to love God and to love their neighbor.

Thanks to some more special friends who have stuck with Anne and me for years: Dave and Karen Beré, John and Claudia Bowen, Carey and Melanie Casey, Gordon and Cheryl Murphy,

Pat and Gretchen McCaskey, John and Peggy Hurt, Dick and Marilyn Lauber, Don and Ann Church, Steve and Martha McNair, Bill and Ann Gahlberg, Bill and Sabra Reichardt, Hub and Joan Erikson, Barbara Beré, Jack and Zondra Swanson, Jan and Marty Pickett, Noel and Marianne Castellanos, John and Vera Mae Perkins, Ron and Nancy Nyberg, and our extended families, the Gordons and the Starkeys.

Thanks to my friend Randy Frame who has helped me to put the right words and sentences together. Randy has a great gift of taking my thoughts and putting them into words that make sense. Randy took the original manuscript from a preaching series and condensed it into these chapters.

Thanks to Bill Greig, Steven Lawson, Mark Weising and all at Regal Books for their tremendous help and faith in this book. Thanks to Alexis Spencer-Byers for working so hard to edit the final manuscript and help me get the final corrections in place.

To contact the author, please write to:

Wayne Gordon
Lawndale Community Church
3827 W. Ogden Ave., Chicago, IL 60623

Or visit the website:

www.lawndalechurch.org